FREEDOM *in* CHRIST

FREEDOM *in* CHRIST

The Way of Truth for the Postmodern Heart

Cindy Casalis
with John S. Knox

foreword by
Kenneth G. Warren

WIPF & STOCK · Eugene, Oregon

FREEDOM IN CHRIST
The Way of Truth for the Postmodern Heart

Wipf & Stock
An Imprint of Wipf and Stock Publishers
199 W. 8th Ave., Suite 3
Eugene, OR 97401

www.wipfandstock.com

PAPERBACK ISBN: 978-1-6667-3889-6
HARDCOVER ISBN: 978-1-6667-3890-2
EBOOK ISBN: 978-1-6667-3891-9

AUGUST 8, 2022 1:56 PM

For my children.

CONTENTS

PREFACE

It seems that even within the Christian's worldview, there is an ever-evolving notion of truth. This is even the case for its very core doctrines. There seems to be disconnect between reaching out to a lost world and being engulfed in its pseudo truths. I began this project as part of my master's thesis. As such, its primary purpose was apologetics. In my studies, I had noticed that the field placed great emphasis on the various ways that the experts approached how to relate the necessity of God from a Christian standpoint. In my eyes, this was a good start, but it required further development of its true significance. That is, I understood that now (more than ever) in a post Postmodern world, people ought to be able to appreciate the meaning of true human freedom.

It is not difficult to see people's incessant pursuit of freedom. Sadly, along the way, they become entrapped in a never-ending chase for materialism or intellectual achievement that leaves them less free than they were at the onset. Ironically, one's earthly achievements become the very constricting chain from which people hoped liberation. Yet, how does this happen, or more importantly, is there a way to avoid it? Is there is biblical basis for this fundament?

The wisest man who even lived acknowledged that money answers everything (Ecclesiastes 10:19, *NKJV*). I realize that this Proverb may be interpreted in many different ways. Yet, it is easy to see how money is a good key to opening doors that may otherwise be inaccessible. Still, there is another opposing possibility that is equally powerful. Namely, that money itself is the reason behind all human events—for better or for worse. People war against each other for the sake of power, which is just another way to refer to money. Once the desired status has been achieved, then those same people become enslaved to it—to the extent that they will do anything and all things to maintain it. It is in this way that the so-called freedom that they originally hoped for has now become their prison.

Although this principle has always been true in society, it was my earnest desire to emphasize it from an apologetic standpoint. There are two related verses from Proverbs and Psalms that shed some light in this reality. In the former, the writer proclaims: "Sheol and Abaddon are never satisfied, and never satisfied are the eyes of man" (Proverbs 27:20, *ESV*). The Psalmist seems to understand this Proverb as he explains: "Deep calls unto deep at the noise of thy waterspouts" (Psalm 42:7, *NKJV*). I realize that these verses are rather profound, but in their simple meaning one may clearly see that they speak of man's insatiable need for acquisition. God's providence has been effectively perverted to this physical world, which was never meant to satisfy the needs of the human soul. Something only God Himself can do.

So, people are left running in circles, placing all their efforts on fruitless endeavors that lead them to their original starting point. My greatest hope for this work is to show that there is a better way to live—one that changes the focus from its circular horizontal path, to an upward one that leads to the very throne of God. More importantly, the message that I want to convey is that this is the ultimate desire of the human heart, and that all others previously mentioned are but a deceptive misrepresentation of the truth.

In other words, true freedom may only be found in the pursuit of God and His truth via adherence to His Word. When Christ read Isaiah 61, this is what He had in mind. It was one of the goals for His ministry. His message went beyond just triumphing over death. The good news means that those enslaved to sin are now effectively free from its oppression.

It is therefore my sincerest hope that all who read this book come to the realization of what Christ has delivered humanity, not only from, but onto. He has delivered those bound by sin onto man's true purpose, the freedom to pursue, and obey God. This is the ultimate expression of freedom. Freedom is not found in the affluence that both knows no bounds and enslaves. Freedom is found sitting next to Lady Wisdom, to the Law of God, and to Christ Himself.

The field of modern Apologetics has much to gain from incorporating these principles into its various disciplines. It is time for the average person, and especially for Christians, to embrace true freedom and give priority to God's commandments rather than to pointless earthly pursuits. In order to accomplish this goal, I begin by attempting to present a better understanding of Psalm 119:45.

From a Christian viewpoint, it might not seem to square with some sections of the New Testament. It declares, "And I will walk in freedom, for I have sought Your precepts." The precepts alluded to are God's Law. Ancient Israel might have not always walked in obedience to their covenant, but this verse illustrates that it was not because they did not know its significance. Once I have expanded on the ancient view of God's Law, my focus shifts to how Christ Himself viewed it (along with His Apostles)—not as a burden, but as a delight.

My heartfelt aspiration for this book is that it would open eyes to the freedom that Christ's sacrifice has afforded—one only found in God's ways. Only then will the endless cycle of people's enslaving daily lives will be broken, opening a new door to living a rewarding life—a life that will accumulate treasures where it really matters, in God's kingdom.

FOREWORD

CASALIS AND KNOX HAVE PROVIDED an in-depth look at one of the more prevalent hot button topics in the life of the church today. This work is also refreshing in that it unpacks what true freedom in Christ represents from a biblical and historical perspective (something that feels lost, at times). This is one of those topics that the wheel does not have to be reinvented because history and Scripture both reveal the answers to the question of "What does freedom in Christ mean for me today?" Freedom in Christ means what it has always meant, it is just that like many other timeless truths, we forget (or we never really knew) what this freedom meant to the patriarchs of the past, what it means for believers right this moment, and what it means for future generations of Christ-followers who could end up in bondage because of their lack of understanding.

The truths shared by Casalis and Knox aid in repudiating false claims or teachings that Christians today might be embracing and interpreting as "freedom in Christ." For example, true Christian freedom does not mean that a believer can claim the name of Christ for salvation and then choose to indulge in those things that are contrary to the scriptures. One would have the "freedom" to make this choice(s), but this could eventually equate to "bondage" rather than "freedom." This would be an example of how a conservative might view someone who is erring in their ideological pursuits of freedom.

Progressives, who may feel they are free to do whatever they find pleasure in life and fulfill this pleasure whenever they wish, may not take kindly to the views of the conservative as they see this approach as something that might cramp their style and love for creature comforts. Of course, the conservative may be thinking of the progressive with thoughts of "What in the world are you doing?" as they ponder the antinomian views of the progressive.

So, which approach is right, and which is wrong? Furthermore, which approach is too rigid and then which approach is too lenient? The battle for these answers rages on and it seems that there is more confusion today than ever before on this topic. In fairness to both schools of thought, Casalis and Knox say neither approach is fully correct, and neither is fully incorrect. This is where Casalis has brilliantly recaptured some important concepts that are truly key to understanding what true freedom in Christ is and where this freedom can be found.

As illustrated above, true freedom can mean different things to different people, but this is where the beauty lies in this work from Casalis and Knox. This work approaches these dynamics in a way that makes the reader search their own soul but does so only after a thorough analysis of the Old Testament Law, the biblical meaning of sin, the concepts of grace, and how both the Law and grace in some ways complement each other. Yes, these still matter, especially if one wants to be free in Christ.

The culminating apologetic (for both progressives and conservatives) presented by Casalis and Knox is that true freedom is found in loving the person of Jesus Christ and Christ alone. As one comes to love the person of Christ better, their position on Christian freedom will naturally become healthier. They will not shun others to the point that they are afraid their interactions with others might lead them into sin, but at the same time, they will choose to maintain their Christian testimony over indulgent decisions that might cause harm to their own reputation. More importantly, they harm the reputation of the One who saved them by giving His life for them on a cross two thousand years ago.

It takes understanding of some of the above concepts to be able to find the appropriate balance of this freedom that Casalis and Knox speak of—and that Scripture teaches. Casalis and Knox have provided this very thorough tool that will assist the casual reader in gaining a better understanding of the many different views of sin, grace, and redemption—but from a practical standpoint, this work will help those seeking the balance mentioned previously that will lead to a life "freedom" in Christ Jesus. This balance will lead to a life that honors God first and foremost but will also lead to a lifestyle in which others can grab hold of this freedom for themselves.

I highly recommend *Freedom in Christ* and I believe it will bring greater clarity to a topic that is not explored today as much as it should be. This work will challenge readers to rethink their own views of Christian freedom, equip believers to help others who may be struggling with freedom and the Christian life, and most importantly, readers will come away with a greater appreciation for Jesus and deeper relationship with Him as the provider of the freedoms discussed in this work.

You will not regret taking the time to read this work, and once engaged, readers will have a difficult time putting this work down.

Dr. Kenneth G. Warren, DMin
Online Psychology Instructor
Liberty University

ACKNOWLEDGEMENTS

I WOULD LIKE TO begin by extending my greatest thanks to Dr. John S. Knox, without whose help this project could not have been accomplished. I am especially thankful for his patience, dedication, guidance, and understanding. His advice was invaluable in all the stages of writing, researching, and formatting the final edition. I (and my family) am eternally indebted to him for all his help and support.

Following, I extend also similar gratitude to Dr. Kenneth Warren who also took the time to read, provide feedback, and so graciously honor me with writing the Foreword. Without both their inputs, this book would not have communicated all its concepts as clearly and succinctly as it does now. I also cannot fail to mention the feedback from all the professors in my Master's in Christian Apologetics degree, of which this work constitutes the pinnacle achievement. They were particularly supportive in the initial stages of the research in terms of guidance and direction.

I should also not forget to thank my supervisor and colleagues from work who were more than happy to allow me the time off to write and focus on the research. They were loving and kind enough to pick up the work in my absence, and for that, much of this work is attributed to them. Serving the insurance needs of Medicare beneficiaries who, in most cases, belong to the more challenged sections of our elderly population, such as those whose finances are specially limited, or those whose health conditions require them to have to rely heavily on external help, serve in a position that is not only physically strenuous, but also emotionally, can be challenging. Their willingness to take over for me in numerous occasions will never be forgotten.

As I dedicate this book to my two beautiful daughters—Samantha and Victoria—who are of the ripe old age of nine and thirteen years old, I extend a heart-felt thank you to them for the many nights they gave up for their mom who was assigned to a computer writing, even if it was in the next room. This work owes them for the many, many times that they did all the house tasks, such as vacuuming, cleaning, dishes, and even cooking dinner. I cannot forget the many times my nine-year-old slept on the couch next to me until I finished, not wanting to leave me alone in the living room. In my eyes, they sacrificed more than I did, and for that I thank them eternally.

Finally, I owe for every word, every helper, every breath, and late night of grace to my God, the Master of the universe, who has allowed me to be a part of His plan of redemption by promoting the truth of His sacred Word. It has been a most humbling experience to write a book that will advance God's mission and plan for humanity. I pray that it may be a blessing to all those who read it, and maybe even inspire others to contribute to the kingdom of God, in any way that Master sees fit. May our beloved Messiah speedily return, in our days.

INTRODUCTION

THE NUMEROUS VIEWS ON the meaning of "freedom in Christ" for His followers can make one wonder whether there is true understanding of it in the church. It is well established that in the liturgical branches of the church, there are several sacraments to be followed, along with many rules that make Christianity almost appear to be a religion of works as opposed to conviction. In contrast, several non-denominational movements—particularly in America—seem to have emerged within the last twenty to thirty years to be the most flexible of all congregational domains, with few-to-almost-no ritualistic activities other than praise, worship, and water immersion.

All the different interpretations of what it means to follow Christ (and to fulfill the Great Commission) bring up questions on how people outside of the church view Christians. If these differences regarding freedom and the Christian walk cause the unreached to be puzzled on church doctrine, then some clarification is necessary. Christians who live their lives in obedience to Christ, and those who understand that the harvest is plenty, but the workers are few, must be able to explain to non-Christians the true meaning of the freedom Christ has purchased. Principally, faithful followers must understand and walk in the way of Christ to be in any position to relay the proper message.

Ostensibly, proper understanding of freedom in Christ directly aids the field of apologetics. If correction is needed on the part of the church, when implemented, a biblical and

Christ-centered church is bound to increase in numbers rather than decrease (Psalm 115:14–15, *KJV*). The promise began in this Psalm, where the LORD promises an increase in numbers to those who fear Him. The promise of increase in this verse is given with the premise of the fear of God. Only then, by fearing God (which translates into following his Word) will increase flourish.

With the aforementioned in mind, the purpose of this book is to find ways to incorporate elements of true freedom in Christ into the field of apologetics. The goal is to present avenues that defenders of the faith (and the entire body of Christ) find useful, supplying relevant answers to those considering the Christian faith. This book further suggests that Christ followers should fully understand the significance of "freedom in Christ" as a gift from God. Then, it will contrast such freedom with the alleged autonomy from religion that the Postmodernists claim. The primary focus noted is the proper goal considering human freedom. In the Postmodern view, freedom exists to facilitate doing as the flesh desires, without limits or boundaries. In the Christian view, the freedom afforded by the Atonement of Christ is for the purpose of serving the Creator.

The Dilemma

As true disciples of the Messiah, the church should be committed to two main endeavors: 1) conforming to the image of Christ, and 2) fulfilling the Great Commission of making disciples. A great objection to Christianity, at least in the postmodern Western world, is that many Christians do not live lives of sanctification.[1] Often hypocritically, their lives are in no way an indication of having been redeemed from the powers of this world; therefore, the outsiders do not understand the point of being a Christian. As Pollack and Pickell point out, "Individuals are increasingly freeing themselves from institutional guidelines in their religious ideas

---

1. Pollack and Pickel, "Religious Individualization," 610.

and behaviors, and thus increasingly making their own decisions about their religion."[2]

Christians must understand that their conduct should be a natural response to the infinite gift of salvation. Furthermore, such understanding should be evident to those around. When it is not, when Christians live fleshly lives or legalistic ones, those outside the church remain skeptical and repulsed. Ultimately, there is no greater apologetic tool than living a life true to Christ.

There is much literature on exegetical research of freedom in Christ.[3] Some discuss the contradictions between Paul's letters and the permanence of the Law of Moses, as if freedom in Christ meant not to follow the love and righteousness the Law implies. Finally, other literature appears to expand the subject of Postmodernism; yet, not enough seems focused on the apologetical aspect of freedom in Christ. Consolidating these ideas would mean that the concept of freedom in Christ has not been sufficiently resorted to in helping to bring people into the kingdom.

Postmodernism seems bound to the ever-changing culture demands,[4] but freedom found in Christ can liberate people from that concealed form of bondage. Today's liberal society aims to attain freedom as its goal. This antinomianism, however, means a lack of all boundaries and license to do as one pleases based on individual preferences. This would imply that in some cases, one has no accountability to society, as long as nobody is harmed. Somewhat ironically, the disciplined Christian life is a result of the gift of faith that delivers true lasting freedom.[5] Christians must have a proper understanding of this liberty to live their lives by it. Freedom, from the Christian perspective, points back to the ability

---

2. Pollack and Pickel, "Religious Individualization," 611.

3. See Frantisek, "Freedom in Christ in Galatians," 235–55; Alexander, "For Freedom," 73–76; Rogers, "Christ's Freedom," 497–512.

4. As Mike Featherstone points out, the current consumer society becomes progressively more variable and less structured by stable norms. Featherstone, *Consumer Culture*, 44.

5. Alexander, "For Freedom," 75.

to abide by the way of life for which Christians believe humans were created—to serve God and to obey Him.

In *The Nature of Atonement: Four Views*,[6] Christ is viewed as victor over the elements of the kingdom of Satan. This sheds light on one aspect of the freedom Christians claims.[7] Christ has won over the dominion that the forces of darkness had over humanity—thereby allowing human existence to return to its original purpose—obedience to God. Additionally, Pauline theology indicates that Christians are free from the Law of Moses to follow Christ and live by faith (Galatians 3:23 and 5:13). Therefore, Christians are free from the Law of Moses and free from slavery to sin, but it is not clear that they are always using this freedom for the right purposes—to build up the body of Christ. Even in the early stages of the church, such as in 1 Corinthians 5, one reads of immorality among the Christians in Corinth, to whom Paul commands putting away the wicked person from them. Clearly, freedom in Christ is not for the purpose of immorality.

If this is due to lack of understanding, then clarification is essential to rectify behavior. With a different interpretation, Dan Lioy, in his book, *Jesus as Torah in John 1–12*,[8] points out that Christ remained faithful to the Law (Galatians 4:4). He continually emphasized its validity in His teachings and went on to expand on its meaning and significance to all people—not just to Israel.[9] The author explains how the believers' relationship to the Law is one of freedom from condemnation.[10] Yet, there is a binding to the timeless moral overarching precepts of God.[11]

The most pervasive worldview found in the Western world is that of Postmodernism. Postmodernism and the idea of freedom from religion has in fact imprisoned individuals to live up to a way

---

6. Beilby and Eddy, *Nature of the Atonement*, 11.

7. Beilby and Eddy, *Nature of the Atonement*, 11.

8. Lioy, *Jesus as Torah*, Chapter 2.

9. Lioy, *Jesus as Torah*, Chapter 2.

10. Lioy, *Jesus as Torah*, Chapter 2.

11. Lioy, *Jesus as Torah*, Chapter 2.

of life that is unattainable.[12] The result is a culture that holds people captive to all its capricious and fleshly demands. The freedom that Christ has purchased for His followers sets people free from that form of enslavement.

Lucy Niall et al. present an insightful paradox of truth. Jurgen Habermas (German sociologist and philosopher, born in 1929) contends that the refusal of reasoning and lack of order of Postmodernism do not allow sufficient grounds for truth.[13] Furthermore, according to Habermas, the achievement of true advancement does not arise from newly revealed truths; instead, from the absence of all foundations, only an ongoing search for truth remains.[14] He asserts, "Rather than abandon truth and reason . . . we should accept that facts emerge through realms of value and intention, and then establish ways of reflecting upon knowledge and human interest."[15]

Researchers have found uneven ground after analyzing the trends in Postmodernism.[16] There is clear opportunity for Christians to approach those who can appreciate the shortcomings of such views. It is against all laws of logic, even without sophisticated analysis, that facts exist—whether they are tangible entities or abstract concepts. Anyone who denies this reality is denying reason itself. On this basis, assertion to the relativity of all things is a similarly dilutional concept. The freedom that the Postmodern embraces is one without boundaries, thereby becoming a danger unto itself. Christian freedom on the other hand, while it is yet liberty, does not defy the laws of logic. Its boundaries do not contradict its identity. Once the proper understanding of freedom in Christ has infused the church, the lives of those truly committed to

---

12. The unattainability meant here refers to idea of always pursuing to keep up with the ever-fluctuating cultural trends that are fast changing and unpredictable.

13. Niall et al., *Dictionary*, 83.

14. Niall et al., *Dictionary*, 83.

15. Niall et al., *Dictionary*, 83.

16. McHale, Cambridge Introduction, 7.

Him will be shine forth. Such change is indispensable to turn the corner on evangelization and apologetics.

Orientation of Freedom

Preliminary findings for this work revealed a general misunderstanding of the doctrine of freedom. Regarding the importance of balance on the matter, it seems best to accept Christ as the one who obeyed the Law of Moses and expanded it. Christians are free from the power of sin. They are to act in love towards all—not to live in lawlessness. Lawlessness, for the church, means not abiding by the law of love. Freedom in Christ means the liberation from the bondage to sin, to be empowered to follow the Laws from the Old Testament, so that the Spirit of God can lead people to obey because of their love for Him and others.

It appears that submission to Christ and His Law is the only appropriate response to the gift of salvation as opposed to earning it. Christians should strictly adhere to at least the Ten Commandments.[17] For instance, take Christ's view on divorce and remarriage in Matthew 5:32. In this verse, Christ is not only dispelling any misunderstandings on this matter, but also doing it under His divine authority. He declares, "It has also been said, 'Whoever divorces his wife must give her a certificate of divorce. But I tell you that anyone who divorces his wife, except for sexual immorality, brings adultery upon her.'" There is no ambivalence on how He feels about this matter. He points to the commandments. Similarly, in Matthew 23:3, Christ tells His disciples to do all the scribes and pharisees tells them to do, but out of love.

On the matter of freedom, Paul's letters must be re-read and studied to gain better understanding. Raisanen and Orton, in

---

17. One could further argue for the inclusion of all the commandments within what Christ calls the greatest commandment in Matthew 22:38: "You shall love your God with all your heart and with all your soul and with all your mind." This sort of love towards the Creator ensures that all other commandments are followed, for who can claim to love the maker of heaven, earth and all that is within it and yet, cheat or steal from his neighbor?

Jesus, Paul and Torah: Collected Essays,[18] point out that Paul seems to be making contradictory statements in relation to the Law. Such contradictions might result from advances in his missionary work. For example, right after declaring the way of salvations to the Romans in chapter 10:9–10, by declaration of Christ' lordship in faith, Paul proceeds to give examples of what the appropriate response is to salvation. In chapter 12:9–21, the reader encounters numerous examples of actions to be taken by those who have just believed. This is an example of love, belief in action. Some could misunderstand such action as a means of salvation. Therefore, Paul is not teaching salvation by such works; yet, he is also not presuming that nothing is to be done.

What is clear, however, is that Paul's experience on the road to Damascus established a clear separation from works of righteousness to righteousness by faith.[19] Menahem Kister, in *Romans 5:12–21 Against the Background of Torah-Theology and Hebrew Usage,*[20] explains how many Jewish concepts played a significant role in Paul's theology. Kister explains: "Many Pauline passages can be illuminated by rabbinic literature."[21] In Romans 5:12–21, where Paul compares Adam to Christ, the parallel is strikingly similar. Rabbi Yose, in the *Sifra,* a piece of rabbinic literature, states, "Therefore, as through one man, sin came into the world and through sin death, and so death came to all men because all men sinned."[22] This passage would be extremely familiar to those who have read the letter to the Romans.

Rabbinic literature sources can aid in understanding Paul's difficult passages.[23] Ian Duffield, in his work, *Difficult Texts: Matthew 28:19–20,*[24] explains how this verse contains a direct command to

---

18. Raisanen and Orton, *Jesus, Paul and Torah,* 18.

19. Raisanen and Orton, *Jesus, Paul, and Torah,* 15.

20. Kister, "Romans 5:12–21," 400.

21. Kister, "Romans 5:12–21," 400.

22. Kister, "Romans 5:12–21," 400.

23. Kister, "Romans 5:12–21," 400.

24. Duffield, "Difficult Texts," 108–11.

the church to teach others Christ' way and the commandments.[25] Duffield in fact declares, "In Matthew, there is a clear call, consistent with the rest of the book, for the Church to teach others (not merely Israel) the way of Christ and to instruct them on how to live by Christ' teaching—His Torah—as supremely expressed in the Sermon on the Mount."[26] This is a call to discipleship more than to the preaching of the Gospel.

In Matthew's Gospel, the will of God is defined in terms of keeping the Law, so explains Thomas Blanton in *Saved by Obedience: Matthew 1:21 in Light of Jesus' Teachings on the Torah*.[27] Therefore, it seems that by living a life of obedience and love, Christians can bring others to Christ. Moreover, before judging others, Christians must understand the views of the secular world. If they do not, they not only fail their mission in this world but fall short of fulfilling the greatest commandment. They need to love God and one's neighbor, for how could one's love be genuine towards another without truly first making an effort to understand their viewpoint?

Notwithstanding, the church must begin with change from within and with boldness in faith. Such faith must be grounded on the belief that Christians are now free to obey God's commandments—in contrast to our position before the Atonement. Before Christ's atoning sacrifice, humans were enslaved by their own sinfulness, making them unable to carry out their service to God as originally intended. This is the purpose for which they were created. However, now, humanity has been restored to the same freedom Adam had before he sinned, still yet able to sin, but not obligated to obey its demands. Therefore, Christians' actions should reflect this understanding with boldness and zeal. Eliminating the church's lukewarmness is a radical change that will deliver clearer and more consistent explanations to those the apologists are trying to win to Christ.

25. Duffield, "Difficult Texts," 108–11.
26. Duffield, "Difficult Texts," 108–11.
27. Blanton, "Saved by Obedience," 405.

1

Is the Law a Burden?

The Meaning of Torah and Sin to the Jews

According to Paul in Romans 7:4–5, Christians hold they have
been freed from the Law: "So, my brothers and sisters, you also
died to the Law through the body of Christ, that you might belong
to another, to Him who was raised from the dead, in order that
we might bear fruit for God." Specifically, in light of John 1:1—"In
the beginning was the Word, and the Word was with God, and
the Word was God"—one must be able to reconcile the eternity
of Christ as the living Word with the concept of being dead to the
Law through the body of Christ (Romans 7:4). Christ clearly explained to His disciples that the outer manifestation of their love
for Him was evident by their adherence to His commandments
(John 14:15).

Sean Burt points out in his article, "The Torah is My Delight,"
in discussing Psalm 119, how even in the poetry of the psalter,
one perceives the devotion and love of the Torah by the Jews.[1]
Christ, being an observant Jew, perfect in every way, would have
been constantly referring to the commandments of the Law. He
affirmed, "Think not that I am come to destroy the Law, or the

---

1. Burt, "Your Torah," 685.

prophets: I am not come to destroy, but to fulfill" (Matthew 5:17, *NKJV*).

To the Jews, the Torah is the Law of life. The Torah brings life and disobedience of it brings death. Therefore, if the fulfilment of the Law is in Christ, then in Him is the fulfilment of life itself. One can easily have better appreciation of the Jews' view of the Law in the following excerpt from the Jewish Women's Daily Prayer Book, a prayer for peace, called *Sim*:

> "Bless us, our Father, all of us as one, with the light of your countenance, for with the light of Your countenance You gave us, HaShem, our God, the Torah of life and a love of kindness, righteousness, blessing, compassion, life, and peace."[2]

From this simple prayer, one can ascertain the Jews' view of the Law—not as a burden but as a delight. The Law shown here is akin to the love of kindness, righteousness, blessing, and compassion (Psalm 119:1–40). The Jews relate to the Law of Moses as a life-giving source—in the same way that Christians relate to Christ as the life-giving Word made flesh. Therefore, for those who love Christ, following His commandments is not burdensome. Obedience is nothing more than a personal manifestation of this love.

It seems hard to believe that Christ would ask His followers to carry out commandments they were unable to execute. This coincides with His response to the rich man who comes to Him inquiring how to obtain eternal life, Christ responds by saying, "Thou knowest the commandments, do not commit adultery, do not kill, do not steal, do not bear false witness." (Luke 18:20, *KJV*). It is important to point out that Christ did not simply reply by admonishing the man to believe in Him and forget about the Law; rather, he reminded the man of its relevance. These are the commandments Christ must have been referring to in John 14:15—not because salvation would come through them, but because honoring them is the same as honoring Christ Himself—the only man through whom salvation comes.

---

2. Scherman and Zlotowitz, *Ohel Sarah*, 89.

Burt points out how the Psalms exhibit the love of the commandments in Torah as a joy.[3] As Burt puts it, "Scholars have made several attempts to delineate the boundaries of Psalm 119's concept of Torah. However, this search for a substantive definition of Torah is misguided because what this text envisions is not a sober-minded instruction, but delight (שעשועים)—to use a term characteristic of the poem."[4] In other words, for those who love the Lord and His Word, following the commandments is not a chain on their necks, but rather a pleasure in their hearts. Daniel Joslyn-Siemiatkoski explains how the giving of both the oral Torah and the written Torah at Mount Sinai is welcomed as a gift of transformation from God to Israel.[5]

Joslyn-Siemiatkoski affirms this notion: "From passages in Mishnah Avot, one can develop a sympathetic reading of the giving of the Torah and Sinai as a transformative gift of God to Israel."[6] Such transformation is in the form of purification for the purpose of priesthood, as mentioned later in Exodus 19:6. The apostle Peter, in the New Testament, mirrors the call to priesthood of the church in 1 Peter 2:9. It is by following the Law that Israel will thrive.[7]

It is important to point out that the Torah was given *after* the deliverance from Egypt, after salvation was provided. One can now clearly see why Moses insisted on the reason why Pharaoh should let the people go— "So that they may worship me" (Exodus 8:1, *NIV*). This teaches that the people were very aware that they were saved by the unmerited favor of God—namely, concerning grace. They understood that following the Law, being a means of worship, is a symbol of gratitude for the salvation already supplied.

Dan Lioy reaffirms the reality that Christ is the culmination of the gift of Torah.[8] He boldly proclaims, "Christ of Nazareth, as

3. Burt, "Your Torah is my Delight," 685.

4. Burt, "Your Torah is my Delight," 685.

5. Joslyn-Siemiatkoski, "Moses Received the Torah," Headnote.

6. Joslyn-Siemiatkoski, "Moses Received the Torah," Headnote.

7. Joslyn-Siemiatkoski, "Moses Received the Torah," 443.

8. Lioy, *Jesus as Torah*, Chapter 8.

the Torah of God, is the reason for deciding to live in such a radical manner. Put another way, the Redeemer is the culmination (that is, the destination, goal, outcome, and fulfillment) of the Law for believers."[9] He reminds the reader that Christ was faithful to it (Galatians 4:4), for he cannot deny Himself (2 Timothy 2:13). He continually emphasized its validity in His teachings and went on to expand on its meaning and significance to all people—not just to Israel.[10]

J. N. Alexander in his work, *For Freedom Christ has Set Us Free*,[11] parallels one of the concepts of freedom's purpose. Alexander puts it this way: "In more ways than we can begin to count, people are bound—bound emotionally, bound spiritually, bound physically—... but it is a bondage they live every moment of every day. And it is the Spirit's desire, God's desire working in us, that they be set free."[12] Commenting on one of the jobs of the priesthood of the Church of Christ, the liberator, he understands the aim of the holy convocation is to set people free to be the people God created them to be.[13] Being free from the bondage in Egypt—by the grace of God—is for the purpose of observing the commands of a loving God.

To take matters a step further, Thomas Blanton in his book, *Saved by Obedience*,[14] concludes that the Gospels depict Christ as a proponent of rigorous observance of the Law.[15] Sin is understood in Matthew to be transgression of the Law—in fact, Matthew 1:21 points to such overarching concept.[16] Christ having reconciled His people to Himself could only mean that He expected them to live how He always had wanted them to live.

---

9. Lioy, *Jesus as Torah*, chapter 8.

10. Lioy, *Jesus as Torah*, chapter 8, chapter 2.

11. Alexander, "For Freedom," 75.

12. Alexander, "For Freedom," 75.

13. Alexander, "For Freedom," 75.

14. Blanton, "Saved by Obedience," Abstract.

15. Blanton, "Saved by Obedience," Abstract.

16. Blanton, "Saved by Obedience," Headnote.

Sin

Defining sin for the ancient Israelite is crucial in understanding the walk of the righteous. It appears that Israel was clear of its implications. Denying the covenant laid out in Deuteronomy is a sign of explicit transgression. To Israel, transgression of the Law is first and foremost transgression against God Himself.

Two significant Scripture passages aid in this understanding. First, Solomon's prayer at the inauguration of the Temple (in his immense wisdom) intercedes for Israel by asking God that when He gives Israel over to his enemies because they have sinned against God—and when they repent—to act justly and to forgive them by bringing them back into the land (1 Kings 8:33–35). This teaches that Solomon expected Israel to have been exiled from the land as a result of transgression of the Law.

Immediately following such supplication, Solomon prays for the ways of the Lord to be taught to the people. If one desires to enter into a restored relationship with God, one must do His will; succinctly, one must respectfully follow His ways. Solomon was aware that the nation of Israel would eventually be mired in sin, and when they did, upon repentance, he appealed to God's mercy. It is as if he was aware that Israel did not yet have the power to overcome sin on her own.

Daniel's prayer represents a similar perspective on Israel's view of sin, perhaps even more indicative of the Jews' understanding of transgression. In Daniel 9:5, he acknowledges Israel's guilt: "We have sinned and committed iniquity, we have done wickedly and rebelled, even by departing from Your precepts and Your judgements." Daniel, a righteous man, beloved by God (Daniel 10:11), interceded on behalf of Israel by acknowledging the sin of the people. First, he recognized that trespassing against God meant not walking in His Law. As a result, the punishment is delivered as promised in the Law of Moses (Daniel 9:13).

In this verse, Daniel speaks of the reliability of the Law when he acknowledged to God that their slavery in exile has been fulfilled in Israel's history, as it is written in the Torah, because of their disobedience. As it is recorded in Deuteronomy 11:13–15, Moses delineates the blessings and curses of Israel's obedience and lack thereof. Obedience leads to blessings, while disobedience leads to banishment from the land.

Christ' proclamation to Israel was that He had come to free them *from* bondage to sin. The message would have been clear to the people. This autonomy was for the purpose of obeying the Law and achieving perfect fellowship with God. Christ admonished His disciples that they should be perfect, for He is perfect (Matthew 5:48). This commandment follows several lines of reasoning. However, the first reference in the Bible to being perfect is perhaps the most important.

God commands Israel to be holy in Leviticus 19:2. The reason that He provides is because God Himself is holy. After all, man was created in the image of God. This is a concept that goes beyond the physical. The reference to being perfect, that is holy, in Matthew 5:48, is more along the lines of loving one's enemies, just as God Himself makes the sun to shine on the righteous and on the wicked alike, as indicated by the preceding verse which states, "And if you greet only your brothers, what are you doing more than others? Do not even Gentiles do the same?"

The Concept of Grace in Judaism

Gil Graff brings to light a contemporary view of the Jews relationship to the Law of God.[17] Graff records the testimony of Leo Jung, a rabbi at the Jewish Center in Manhattan in 1922. Graff writes, "For Jung, living as a Jew meant the pursuit of ethical perfection through the study and practice of Torah: The words 'justice, righteousness, freedom' are the eternal refrain of Jewish teaching and Jewish living."[18] After all the time that had passed since Christ' first coming, little had changed. The Jews, as a people, might have rejected their Messiah; however, they have not rejected His Law.

17. Graff, "Giving Voice," 167.
18. Graff, "Giving Voice," 172.

Graff records the words of the Rabbi: "We must intensify our allegiance . . . to the Law of God which gives us dignity and destiny."[19] Interestingly, the teacher speaks of justice, righteousness, and freedom as the eternal code of Judaism.[20] Regardless of how many times the Old Testament represents Israel as the unfaithful wife, it was not for lack of understanding of what it meant to be "faithful."

It is important to point out—based on the rabbi's assertion—that freedom is directly associated with the Law of God. This seems a paradoxical statement. In the Jewish view, true freedom is being able to perform what the Law says. Consequently, bondage is the inability of obedience. It appears that this concept defines freedom to those who follow the greatest Jew who ever lived (and lives)—Christ. God has used the Jews' initial rejection of their Messiah to open His kingdom to the rest of all nations and tongues. However, one must not forget that Christianity is a sect of Judaism, the religion of the Messiah.

The biblical Christian view of freedom does not explicitly deny the Law of the Old Testament. However, nor does it call for strict adherence to it. The biblical verse that best exemplifies Christians' freedom is Galatians 5:13, *KJV*: "For, brethren, ye have been called unto liberty; only use not liberty for an occasion to the flesh, but by love serve one another." Love for God and one another is the essence of God and the Law itself, but what does that mean, practically? The answer is a combination of all responsible interpretations of the New Testament letters and of the Gospels, themselves.

Christians believe that grace is that by which humanity now lives. Despite popular belief, both Christians and Jews understand that they live under grace. As it is written in Romans 6:14, *NIV*: "Sin shall not be your master, because you are not under Law, but under grace." Chilton and Evans point to the writings of Rabbi Ishmael who indicates that a person, in his efforts to be like God, should imitate God's grace and mercy.[21] This points to grace being

19. Graff, "Giving Voice," 173.
20. Graff, "Giving Voice," 173.
21. Chilton and Evans, *Practice*, 148.

15

paramount in Jewish thought. Considering that Israel was delivered from Egypt by the grace of God and because of His promise to their forefathers, it seems logical that the Jewish sages speak of grace in the following way.

Rabbi Hama asks, "What is the meaning of the Scripture; 'You shall walk after the Lord your God' (Deuteronomy 13:5)"?[22] According to his interpretation, to walk in the ways of the Lord is to show grace. Such grace is manifested by the clothing of the naked, the visiting of the sick, the comforting of mourners, among others. These are all concepts that Christians see mirrored in the New Testament. Such instruction, often coming directly from Christ and other times from Paul, also gives a good definition of grace towards all people as a sign of love. God has saved His children by His grace, so should they extend grace to others as a sign of their love.

Christians are meant to love others because they have been saved by God's grace through their faith and their appreciation in Him (Ephesians 2:8–9). Such salvation points to obedience in love of God and His people. For those who love God, whether Jews or Christians, grace means the same. It means unmerited favor from a God of unending mercies. Therefore, His commandments are not burdensome—they are a pleasure.

Following God's instructions is for the person's own benefit. People are privileged to be participants along with the legions of heaven in singing praises to God. James, the brother of Christ, reminds the reader in his letter not to merely look at the Word, but to do what it says (James 1:22). This is the true meaning of faith (James 1:25).

The commandments written in the Law, and those prompted by the Spirit of the Lord living in the believer, are not a burden. Furthermore, the Spirit of holiness now endowed in Christians overcomes the evil inclination by making it subservient to God. In the same way, the Jews are in love with the Law; true Christians are in love with God and all people. This love brings freedom, not

---

22. Chilton and Evans, *Practice*, 149.

bondage. For example, one can never be prevented from loving. This might seem like an outlandish statement; yet, it truly is not.

The greatest demonstration of love was Christ's sacrifice on the Cross. No one could interfere with this manifestation of His love for humanity. The same is true when a parent chooses to be by his child's side while he pays the consequences of some wrong action. This is because of the parent's love. No person can interfere with this action of love. In this way, there is true freedom in loving.

The Law and Grace to the Jews of Today

For the Jews, obedience to the Law stems from their election by God.[23] However, within Judaism, there are many ways of interpreting how to walk the faith. Some Jews accept upon themselves more stringent walks than others. Some believe that the Messiah has already come, but not Christ, such as Chabad Jews. Others who ascribe to Reformed Judaism do not acknowledge the existence of a literal Messiah at all. Of course, there are those who believe that Christ is the Messiah. Yet, all are counted within Judaism, although they have very distinct walks.

In the same way that Christianity has separated into several denominations, so does Judaism have more strict observant denominations. Those who chose to not observe the Law of Moses, such as Reformed Jews, will not be addressed in this work since they do not estimate observance as an obligation. Those who do, such as Orthodox Jews, their stringency often suggests to outsiders that they observe for the sake of salvation. This assertion must be explained further.

What is being said is not that present-day Judaism does not understand that their salvation is by unmerited grace; rather, that their observance appears to the world as fear of falling away from the grace of God. In other words, to Jews, Torah observance is not for the purpose of salvation, but it is the suitable response to God's grace and the salvation already provided, although to outsiders it

23. Tapie, "Christ, Torah," 17.

might seem like a works' salvation religion. Perhaps this is a simplistic judgement of Judaism by the goyim (non-Jews).

Truly, the strict observance of the Law of Moses comes across in some cases as archaic, unrealistic, and impractical. Visiting Jerusalem today—and other Jewish communities around the world—is an experience that might leave some feeling this way. Public transportation (along with most motorized vehicles) does not operate during Shabbat. Most (if not all) places of business are closed starting on Friday afternoon until sundown on Saturday.

During the different biblical festivals observed by the Jews, extreme measures take place all over the world by communities who discard all leaven food from their homes to celebrate the Feast of Unleavened Bread, for example. There are Jews today who do not eat fish or meat because of Talmudic input on the possibility of leprosy.[24] Clearly, traditions in this sect of Judaism supersede recent scientific discoveries that contest this assumption. Furthermore, Allen points out that tradition seems to have a stronger impact in some denominations than the modern prospect of discerning matters, like who is a true son of Aaron the brother of Moses.[25] He writes, "According to Rabbi Parnes, there can never be a time when the Torah must yield to scientific discoveries since the principles of the Torah are eternally true and immutable."[26]

Alternatively, Orthodox Judaism is opened to ongoing critical criticism of the Bible. Websites such as TheTorah.com aim to make modern scriptural scholarship available to all Jews, to integrate modern scholarship and to address challenges of current interpretations of traditions and observance.[27] Paradoxically, Judaism has always been a religion where open-mindedness and critical thinking are encouraged—yet, tradition and misunderstandings are so strong and prevalent that most of the outside world perceives them as a religion of works.

---

24. Allen, "Liberal Movements," 48.
25. Allen, "Liberal Movements," 48.
26. Allen, "Liberal Movements," 48.
27. Ferziger, "Fluidity and Bifurcation," 233–70.

2

CHRIST'S FREEDOM AND SIN

The Concept of Freedom to the Progressive Christian

REGARDING PROGRESSIVE CHRISTIANITY, one must first look at its biblical basis. Progressive Christianity is more than just a simple misinterpretation of Scripture. Instead, it represents a combination of political and social ideas that are continually finding their way into society via religion. Although Christians are shifting from conservative to more liberal ideals,[1] Christianity is still considered a conservative religion. It might be difficult to determine whether Christianity, as an institution, is in fact becoming more tolerant, as it were, or if such trends are to be attributed to grass roots movements. Perhaps the fair assessment is a combination of the two. John Williams summarizes this idea as follows:

> Global Christianity might be evolving imaginative ways of redefining Christian authenticity and sustaining Christian practice in situations of social and cultural challenge . . . frequently emerging from young or marginalized groups who are putting sharp questions to the

1. Williams, "Christianity in the Modern World," 87–89.

guardians of orthodoxy that are not being taken with adequate seriousness.[2]

The organization Progressive Christians Uniting defines itself as follows: (A) Approach to God through the life of Christ, (B) Recognize that others have different ways to God, (C) Invite all people to participate in their community without insisting in their conversion. They include agnostics, skeptics, men, and women, all sexual orientations and identities, all races, and identities, and so on. Finally, (D) Finding more grace in the research for understanding than in dogmatic certainty. Among other listed definitions, for a total of eight.[3]

According to Edles, this movement was born of a sect that challenged prominent political and religious traditions.[4] Edles states, "This celebration of religious pluralism, indeterminacy and inclusivity is a not-so-subtle jab at conservative Christianity's notorious 'dogmatic certainty' that salvation (and Holy Communion) is not for those of other faiths (let alone those of no faith); and homophobia."[5] In these cases, the movement has already surpassed a basic grassroots level and achieved a higher status. That is not to concede either to the validity nor to the error of their theological views; rather, they are to be examined as a group of people who aim to be understood, heard, and responded to properly not from a simple stance of tolerant superficial love, but from a sincere, actionable, and biblically based love.

Upon analyzing these Christian views, one wonders whether these believers misunderstand the power of God or whether they are responding out of disgust for genuine injustice towards those they are wanting to welcome to their community. Their parameters seem contradictory. If, however, those Christians are responding out of a heart of compassion for their neighbors who are being oppressed and discriminated against (such as is the case against

---

2. Williams, "Christianity in the Modern World," 89.

3. Edles, "Contemporary Progressive Christianity," 3–22.

4. Edles, "Contemporary Progressive Christianity," Theological Background.

5. Edles, "Contemporary Progressive Christianity," Theological Background.

outcasts and skeptics), then their actions are commendable. No one could deny that Christianity calls for compassion and hospitality. However, it is not clear in their declarations that those Progressive Christian branches fully understand the power of God, nor the meaning of truly helping others.

If one believes that being an agnostic or a skeptic is a healthy state of mind, then there is no reason to help anyone. This is what seems to be what is happening. Yet, anyone who has experienced the peace of God would admit that being a skeptic corners a person into a rather miserable position. A double-minded individual simply does not have peace. As it is written, "And the peace of God, which transcends all understanding, will guard your hearts and minds in Christ Jesus" (Philippians 4:7, NIV).

Christians should unapologetically follow biblical instruction regarding those whose lifestyle is not becoming. Yet, they should support people of all backgrounds and ideologies, not to force Christianity upon them; rather, in love, patience and mercy, they should help people see the truth of God and His good will for their lives. Christians should remain steadfast regarding the absolute truths of the Bible and respond properly to those who deny its metanarratives.

The Sadducees were a sect of Judaism at the time of Christ who could be considered today a parallel to Progressive Christianity. Among other assumptions, for example, they did not believe in the Resurrection, nor did they honor the oral Torah. They were, in fact, the secular priests belonging to the Sanhedrin at the time of Christ (Acts 23:8).

In their efforts to test the Messiah, they asked Him a question regarding the resurrection of the dead. They present the scenario of a wife who has married seven brothers upon their successive deaths. Christ is asked whose wife would she be at the final resurrection. Some would say His response could be a fitting one for a Progressive Christian. Christ explained to the Sadducees that their misjudgments stemmed from both, not only their ignorance of the Scriptures, but also of the power of God (Matthew 22:29).

It could be the case for Progressive Christians that the power that God has to change hearts is not fully understood. It could be that it is not understood that God accepts all, and yet, Christ expects them to change for the better by adhering to biblical guidelines. The love of God does not mean tolerance or permissiveness. Instead, the Scriptures are clear regarding the lifestyles that the Lord does not tolerate—and also the power the Lord has to change all people. Therefore, their view, as self-contradictory is the best way to describe antinomianism (against the law), a view to which most Progressive Christians ascribe.

It is succinctly put as follows: "The entire Mosaic Law comes to fulfillment in Christ . . . Christian behavior is now guided directly by 'the Law of Christ.' This 'Law' does not consist of legal prescriptions . . . but of the guiding influence of the indwelling of the Holy Spirit."[6] The contradiction rests in that the promptings of said Holy Spirit cannot go against what is written in the Law of God. As it is written in John 1:1–2, "In the beginning was the Word, and the Word was with God, and the Word was God. He (meaning Christ) was with God in the beginning."

Ultimately, the greatest danger (according to Edles) is that this type of Christianity ignores the need for Christians to be inwardly transformed.[7] This is part of the self-contradiction of the movement; namely, being rescued from sin yet making special pleading for its continuance. Yet, that attitude is clearly judged in the Bible. As Paul calls out in Romans 6:1, "Shall we go on sinning so that grace may abound? By no means." The life of Jesus, corroborated by Paul the apostle, exemplifies a life of transformation towards holiness. This holiness was not attainable, at least to the level that it is now, before Christ's sacrifice. It is the potential of continuing holiness that humans are now freed to pursue in a redeemed life.

The renewal of the mind that Paul was referring to in Romans 12:2 is not one towards the ways of the world,[8] but away from

6. Bahnsen and Vangemeren, *Law, the Gospel*, 376.

7. Edles, "Contemporary Progressive Christianity," 4.

8. As exemplified by the life and martyrdom of Polycarp, who coined the concept of *Imitatio Christi*. In his life and death, the Christian bishop of

them, towards the Scriptures. Paul was speaking in Romans to a former pagan community, not to observing Jews. Therefore, the renewal of the mind was for the purpose of looking to Christ, the Word made flesh. One can appreciate the importance of the use of the mind emphasized here in Scripture.

In contrast to popular belief, the Bible does not foment blind faith; rather, the mind is used to point to God and His Word not away from it. It appears that Progressive Christians are using the mind—yet, in the opposite direction that God has intended. Paul points in this passage to the perfect will of God using the renewed mind. The question is whether God wants Christians involved in political movements, or social justice.[9] Conservative Christians would agree that these matters are not part of the church's great commission.

The movement of Progressive Christianity in many ways also appears to have emerged from grass roots movements.[10] In other words, these trends are emerging from lay groups within and outside the church. It is debatable whether these trends are a result of the church's lack of embrace of all the issues that matter to her members. It appears that the key is that the church is to aim for greater balance at both understanding and executing her responsibilities in caring for the people of God.

Conroy explains how Progressive Christians embrace spirituality and emotional depth.[11] More importantly, they emphasize a liberal heritage of social justice and affirmation of all types of lifestyles. Finally, they focus on the part Christians play in the role of caring for the environment. He explains, "These churches also possess a distinctive concern for the environment, for the

---

Smyrna mimicked the actions of Christ's own life and death to the extent that the idea of *Imitatio Christi* has become a staple among students of early Christian martyrdom. The bases of Polycarp's actions are that Christians are not permitted to act any less morally or spiritually, or at least to aim for, the holiness and example of Christ Himself. See Hartog, "Christology of the Martyrdom of Polycarp," 137–52.

9. Conroy, "New Spiritual Home," 169–70.

10. Conroy, "New Spiritual Home," 169–70.

11. Conroy, "New Spiritual Home," 169–70.

full affirmation of women and lesbian/gay/bisexual persons, and the respect for and even willingness to learn from other religious traditions."[12]

In other words, Progressive Christians understand the need to love all people without eternally judging them. They understand the need to care for others; yet, their love does not truly represent the life of a transformed individual. This can only be accomplished by the power of God. Bringing people into the kingdom is only the first step.

It would be safe to say that for this new sect of Christians, freedom in Christ means being accepted into the kingdom of God without the process of transformation (or confession or repentance or conscience). Such an acceptance gives the concept of freedom in Christ an erroneous view of partial significance. As proposed previously, freedom in Christ is for the purpose of being who God intended people to be. As it is written in Galatians 5:13, "For you, brothers, were called to freedom; but do not use your freedom as an opportunity for the flesh. Rather, serve one another in love."

In case there is any doubt on what the works of the flesh are, Paul goes on to enumerate them: "Now the works of the flesh are evident: sexual immorality, impurity, sensuality . . . I warn you, as I warned you before, that those who do such things will not inherit the kingdom of God" (Galatians 5:19–21, *ESV*). Therefore, there is no biblical basis for tolerance of those who unrepentantly embrace these behaviors.

According to the Bible, God wants all to be saved and none to perish (1 Timothy 2:4), and for all to live up to the standards set in Scripture. The precepts shown in Scripture signify the primary revelation of God's requirements and expectations from all people. He does not want people to eternally condemn one another; instead, they are to admonish one another to follow the path to righteousness in love—for the sake of sanctification of the body of Christ. Freedom in Christ does not mean that people can set their own standard or rules to live by, particularly if they entail continuing to sin, freely.

12. Conroy, "New Spiritual Home," 169–70.

Moreover, Paul declares, "Do you not know that the wicked will not inherit the kingdom of God? Do not be deceived: Neither the sexually immoral, nor idolaters, not adulterers, nor men who submit to or perform homosexual acts" (1 Corinthians 6:9, *BSB*). Therefore, Progressive Christians cannot logically claim that they approach God through the life or model of Jesus Christ; all the while being opened to accept all without condoning anyone on their list. It is an undeniable contradiction.

Paul O'Callaghan brings up an important point that could help the church understand its identity first and foremost. He explains:

> Things get more complex however when temperamentally conservative or liberal individuals get involved in society or politics or economics or education or religion or activities of any other kind. Political, social, economic, and religious positions are easily labelled 'conservative' or 'liberal' on the basis of the personality types of those who support them and the positions they hold. The collective or public actions they carry out with the support and encouragement of like-minded persons take on the liberal or conservative profile of those involved. And so there arises a conservative or a liberal political programme, a conservative or liberal educational or economic policy, a conservative or liberal religion and so on.[13]

This point could be beneficial in finding the balance that would prevent some members of the church from feeling the need to start subgroups through which they feel more appropriately represented. O'Callaghan has explained how a Christian might be in nature conservative or liberal, yet his identity calls him to be both, paradoxically.[14]

A believer can be liberal at understanding his position before salvation and embrace the new brothers and sisters as they are. O'Callaghan explains how Christians love people as individuals with the intent of improving the world and its people. This

13. O'Callaghan, "Is the Christian Believer," 141.
14. O'Callaghan, "Is the Christian Believer," 141.

obligates them to approach brothers and sisters with a "liberal" mindset. At the same time, Christianity must not compromise on its core values. Values of sanctification and transformation, of patience, real admonishing love, of understanding, can keep a person balanced while yet retaining his identity.

Comparably, the concept of Christian Humanism is founded on a gnostic Christology that views the Gospels as mythical and mysterious—particularly concerning the deity of Jesus.[15] This is being brought up because it is yet another sign of the symptoms—as it were—of Progressive and Humanistic Christianity. Herein is the definition of heresy: to not believe in the fundamental doctrines of Christianity.

Augustine himself defines heresy very insightfully when he states, "Those in the church of Christ who crave some unhealthy and base opinion, and who on being reproved, so that they may relish sound and right opinions, stubbornly resist and are unwilling to reform their pernicious and deadly dogmas but persist in defending them."[16] Therefore, it can safely be concluded that the emergence of these trends within the church is not only a result of its lack of or greater involvement in non-religious areas of importance to the community, but ultimately as a result of their relinquishment of the Word of God.

A church that acknowledges that her disciples need to see greater involvement in environmental matters (along with showing greater compassion and acceptance as a first step to other members of the community) is sure to drastically lower the rise of movements that step outside of the boundaries of God's Word. This is not to say that the church is a governmental or fundamentally humanitarian organization; rather, as part of the community, it should honestly reconsider what role it plays in such matters.

15. De Gruchy, "Christian Humanism," 69.
16. Augustine, *City of God*, 18.

The Concept of Freedom to the Conservative Modern Christian

Freedom in conservative Christianity appears to be a more complicated concept to illustrate. Conservative Christianity seems to be more concerned with the volitional absence of sinning. In many ways, conservative Christianity comes across to many as Orthodox Judaism does—a religion of works. Again, this point must be carefully explained to avoid misunderstanding.

In most cases, fear of sin in the walk of a Christian comes across as fear of falling from God's grace, even if unintended by the individual. After all, the ultimate goal of remaining biblically faithful is the love of others. This is not to undermine a pious person's faithfulness; rather, it is to point out the world's perception of them. What is in many cases mistakenly labelled as fundamentalism, rather than love of people, can ironically lead to self-righteousness and lack of godly love.

In fact, fundamentalism is viewed in such opposition to the progressive schema that Paul Maltby infers the following:

> Whereas the fundamentalist worldview remains committed to Biblical literalism, metaphysical dualism, and a conservative social agenda, the postmodern outlook derives from what some critical theorists have called anti-foundationalism, insisting on the historical contingency of all texts, including Scripture, and indeed of all persons.[17]

The point to be made is that contingent upon the opposition of spectrums between fundamentalism and the sensitivity of postmodern culture, as described above, if progressives' embrace tolerance and permissiveness, then fundamentalists adhere to the opposite attitude. This is what is seen as lack of love.

The fundamentalist's approach can be both a curse and a blessing. It can be a blessing because it opens the door to following a life of righteousness and holiness—as long as it does not hinder loving others. It is true (and biblically evidential) that the Lord has

---

17. Eaton, "Review of *Christian Fundamentalism*."

called His people to be holy because He is holy (1 Peter 1:16, *KJV*). People should pursue a life that abstains from even the appearance of evil. How then can one become all things to all people so that by all possible means some can be saved?

Without balance, the blessings of a life of righteousness becomes a curse and slavery. Being careful in defining balance, its meaning can be clarified by the following analogies. One might have a piece of cake, but not the whole cake. Similarly, it is acceptable to have fun at a comedy show, as long it is not at the expense of others' dignity and reputation. Here, one is reminded of the example above referring to what some would call the extreme measure of not allowing elevators to function during the Sabbath day in the Holy Land. It can be argued that in no way boarding an elevator on the Sabbath violates the mandate of abstaining from all labor as described in Exodus 20: 8–11 (*NIV*):

> Remember the Sabbath day by keeping it holy . . . On it you shall not do any work, neither you, nor your son or daughter, nor your male or female servant, nor your animals, nor any foreigner residing in your towns. For in six days the LORD made the heavens and the earth, the sea, and all that is in them, but He rested on the seventh day.

In this way, the commandment has become a curse. One might ponder how so. A person who needs to get to the 10th floor of a building must now take the stairs.

One cannot be so heavenly minded that he or she is disconnected from this world where he has been given the mission to be fishers of men. It is impractical to be so focused on strict rules, and not allowing occasion to care for the needs of others whom people are commanded to love. For as in the case of the elevator example, if the purpose of the visit to him who lives on the tenth floor was to help, particularly in a lifesaving circumstance, the support might be hindered by a helper's inability to hike to the tenth floor.

Fundamentalism falls in the category of self-refuting when it condemns others who do not live up to their standards. Consequently, people's insistence on following a set of rules, for example, close-mindedness to new ideas, lack of flexibility, and critical thinking is counter intuitive to a faith that seeks evangelism and outreach. Religious intensity and strict adherence to the Canon are but some of the terms that describe fundamentalism.[18] However, this is not where the main problems lie, primarily. Rather, the greatest danger of hyper-fundamentalism is that it estranges and condemns people.

This is not to say that all rules can be disregarded to bring people into the covenant, while they continue to sin as before. For the same man who said, "To the weak, I became weak, to win the weak. I have become all things to all people so that by all possible means I might save some (1 Corinthians 9:22, *BSB*)," also said, "Do not copy the behaviors and customs of this world, but let God transform you into a new person by changing the way you think. Then you will learn to know God's will for you, which is good and pleasing and perfect" (Romans 12:2, *NLT*). Instead, compassion, mercy, and love should be principal. Christ promised a life of transformation for those coming into the family of God and for those whose preconceived ideas—even religious ones—are hindering them from becoming all God wishes them to become, for the sake of the kingdom.

Gospel's Teachings on Freedom

Christ's words on freedom establish the foundation for true Christian liberty. The key is to appreciate the prison from which Christ has freed humanity. In other words, upon careful examination of John 8:31–36, one is enlightened to Christ's perspective. As it is written:

> To the Jews who had believed him, Jesus said, "If you hold to my teaching, you are really my disciples. Then you will know the truth, and the truth will set you free. They answered him, "We are Abraham's descendants and have never been slaves of anyone. How can you say that we shall be set free?" Jesus replied, "Very truly I tell you, everyone who sins is a slave to sin. Now a slave has no

18. Epstein and Gang, "Understanding the Development," 257–71.

permanent place in the family, but a son belongs to it forever. So, if the Son sets you free, you will be free indeed.

Darrell Bock explains how John, in his Gospel, presents the sending of the only Son of God who brings blessing and life.[19] He states, "In relation to the second commandment, Christ is the very image of the Father (Colossians 1:15), the only mediator between God and man (1 Timothy 2:5), and the supreme mediator of revelation, presence and worship."[20] Christ presents freedom from slavery to sin unto life. Those who follow Christ are the sons of God. Those who do not follow Christ are not. Therefore, freedom in John's Gospel is to follow Christ's teachings and His Word, according to John 8:31–32.

Christ explains how those who hold to His teaching are His disciples. Only then, they shall know the truth that sets free. To know the truth is to know Christ, as it is written, "I am the way, the truth, and the life" (John 14:6, *KJV*). Once someone becomes Christ's disciple, then he or she is in a position to know Him, personally. This knowledge of Christ is the very thing that ushers in freedom from sin. This freedom from sin means no longer being subservient to the evil inclination of the human soul.

In Luke's Gospel, a similar concept of freedom in Christ is portrayed. Luke 4:18 groups together freedom with spiritual healing (and release from oppression). Bondage to sin is akin to oppression and captivity. It appears that it is not only in these first two Gospels, but the overarching theme of all is to proclaim freedom from slavery to sin into salvation manifesting through obedience to God's Word. It is written, "Ye shall know them by their fruits" (Matthew 7:16–23, *KJV*).

It is debatable that a true child of God, through the renewed covenant instituted by the blood of Christ, is so much more controlled by his evil inclination than by the fruits of his or her actions that do not belong to the kingdom of God. It is not a that a believer, once saved, never commits a sin again. Instead, it is that his life is

---

19. Block, *Israel: Ancient Kingdom*, 325.
20. Block, *Israel: Ancient Kingdom*, 325.

a greater portrayal of the life of Christ Himself, than it is of the life of the world (or the lives of unbelievers). As 1 John 4:4 states, "The one who is in you is greater than the one who is in the world."

Therefore, paradoxically, a true believer in Christ is known by his righteous actions, as long as they glorify God and not the individual himself. This is the Gospel's meaning of Christian freedom, according to John 8:31–36. It is freedom from the ways of the world onto freedom to embrace the good, eternal, beneficial ways of God.

It is paramount to remember that the Holy Spirit's ability to bring this sort of freedom is an indication of His identity in relationship to God. For it is inconceivable to accept that one can claim the freedom of God without the indwelling of His Spirit. For it is only through Him that one can claim triumph over his evil inclination. The Holy Spirit is Himself the witness to the freedom of Christ, just as the spirit of the world is a witness to its oppression and bondage. For this reason, Christ was accused of blasphemy and condemned by the Jews, because they knew that only God could offer this kind of freedom.

By asserting the words of Isaiah 61:1, Christ was proclaiming Himself as equal to God.[21] Christ's declarations are a witness to 1 John 4:4, thereby testifying to the superiority of the Spirit of God over the spirit of the world. For if indeed the spirit of the world oppresses people, then only the strength of a more powerful Spirit can declare rulership over him.

The Nature of the Atonement

The concept of atonement is of greater implications than most realize. The liberation and triumph afforded to humanity permeate into several levels of human existence. The defeat of Satan, the freedom from sin, the possibility of reconciliation with a Holy God, spiritual and bodily healing, are but a few victories. No wonder that the concept of mending a wrong, to atone, is used to label

21. Pancaro, *Law in the Fourth Gospel*, 56.

Christ's work. It is not until an action is taken to revert a wrong, that the offended party is able to accept—"payment," as it were—for the sin. One can simply say that they are sorry, but it is not until an action is intentionally taken supporting that sentiment that the offended party believes in the true repentance of the offender.

The Nature of Atonement: Four Views brings to light the major implications of Christian freedom.[22] As with any thorough scriptural analysis, context is essential. One of the biggest objections to Christ's title of "The Prince of Peace" is that this world (just as in biblical times) does not have peace. The misunderstanding lies in the perception that through Christ's first coming all His plans would be accomplished, one of which was ushering world peace. Thankfully, the spiritual peace imparted to the believer can be experienced now, in this life; yet, world peace is reserved only for the world to come.

The victory of Christ's Atonement is strategically placed against the background of intense spiritual warfare. Christ was very clear in who the two kingdoms at war were—then and still now (Mark 3:24–26, Matthew 12:22–28). Today, as the flesh still battles with the spirit that seeks God, believers can rest in the assurance that the war is won over the agents of evil. The Hebrew Scriptures are replete with warfare references and terms.

God is commonly known in the Hebrew texts as the Lord of heaven's armies and a God of war (Psalm 24:7–9, 82). So, it is no surprise that Christ makes many warfare references in His Gospels. The ancient Jewish view of the earth as warfare ground between spiritual forces of evil and good, influenced their understandings of natural disasters and even illness (1 Chronicles 21). Therefore, Christ's main objective was to regain the world that Satan deceitfully stole from God.[23]

This is not in any way to insinuate that God has not been in control of all the creation at any given point in history. Rather, it highlights God's respect for human's free will, their choices and His resistance to commune with sinful beings. In this way, Christ's

22. Beilby and Eddy, *Nature of Atonement*, 23.
23. Wilkens, *Faith and Reason*, 28.

triumph over the actions of Satan eliminated his subjugation of humanity. Christ is then able to give all power over the forces of the kingdom of Satan to believers.

The second concept of the atonement falls in the arena of legal matters. Many overlook the legal nature of the Scriptures as an official document, a testament. Usually, when one is preparing to have one redacted, he seeks the assistance of a legal agent, an attorney for instance. The statements made by any king in ancient times (and even today) cannot be retracted; therefore, they are binding, in the same sense as legal decrees are.

God could not retract His decrees written in the Law of Moses; a renewal agreement was necessary without compromising the justice of God. This understanding of authority and kingship is seen in Ahasuerus' original decree to annihilate all Jews.[24] His decree could not be retracted; yet, an amendment could be issued. To the queen's petition, the king responded, "Write ye also, as it liketh you, in the king's name, and seal it with the king's ring: for the writing, which is written in the king's name, and sealed with the king's ring, may no man reverse" (Esther 8:8, *KJV*).

Thomas R. Schreiner stresses the foundational importance of the penal substitution that took place in Golgotha.[25] He asserts, "The governmental theory of the atonement emphasizes that God desires to show how seriously He takes the Law without requiring a full payment for every infraction . . . God's Law needs to be honored in order for sinners to be forgiven."[26] A penal system would necessitate the involvement of a guilty party. Humans are not victims of their actions, but they willingly give in to the tempter. Schreiner points out how the governmental connotation of the Atonement is an indication of the value God gives to the Law. It is no wonder Christ affirms that not one jot or tittle of the Law will

---

24. After Haman, the enemy of the Jews was hanged, Esther the Queen pleaded with King Ahasuerus to reverse the original decree to annihilate all Jews in his kingdom.

25. Beilby and Eddy, *Nature of Atonement*, 68.

26. Beilby and Eddy, *Nature of Atonement*, 68.

be changed. So, in many ways, the Atonement is viewed by God and by those who are able to grasp it, as a legal transaction.

Perhaps the most misunderstood facet of the Atonement is the healing aspect. It is debatable whether believers and non-believers alike fully understand the double prospect of healing— spiritual and bodily. This is a concept the Christ assumed people understood when he asked Nicodemus: "Art thou a master of Israel, and knowest not these things?" (John: 3:10, *KJV*). The understanding was that while there are natural aspects to life, in many cases, they parallel spiritual ones—e.g., birth and healing. Healing was something that Israel understood to only come from God, just as freedom from slavery to sin did (Isaiah 57:17–19).

Bruce R. Reichenbach points to how, biblically speaking, healing was not possible until there was fulfilment of the Law, in this case, vis a vis Christ's Atonement (Isaiah 58:8).[27] For spiritual and even physical sickness is a direct result of transgression. This is what was written in the Law. As it states in Exodus 15:26, *NKJV*, "If you diligently heed the voice of the Lord your God and do what is right in His sight, give ear to His commandments and keep all His statutes, I will put none of the diseases on you which I brought on the Egyptians. For I am the Lord who heals you."

God could not simply wave the consequences of human action. He cannot take back His Word. Whether someone is prepared to accept it or not, God does cause sickness directly and indirectly due to what is written in the Law.[28] Israel was quite aware of this fact, so for Christ to claim that He could restore healing was to simply claim equality with God.

The Atonement of Christ on humanity's behalf was a complete reversal of the curses that they were under since the Fall. Humanity was in a state of humiliation; therefore, Christ was personally humiliated so that people could be exalted. He was dishonored so people could be honored. He was ridiculed so that people could be extolled. He was insulted so that people could be praised. He was wounded so that people could be healed. He was abandoned by

27. Beilby and Eddy, *Nature of Atonement*, 118.
28. Beilby and Eddy, *Nature of Atonement*, 121.

God, so that people could be reconciled to Him (Matthew 27:46). Finally, He accepted condemnation so people could be free to walk with God again—some would argue as man was meant to walk with God before the fall of humanity. This is the essential nature of the Atonement.

Alternative Views

At this point, it is important to address alternative views to the traditional definition of Christianity. In *Jesus, Paul and The Torah*, the authors present a slightly different view of Paul's relationship to the Law.[29] Raisanen and Orton argue how, for example, in Romans 3:27, there has been traditionally a connection made to "the Law of works," and the Torah itself. In other words, when Paul refers to working, performing the commandments, this is equaled to living under the Law of Moses. However, in the same way that the church has recently seen a shift to Progressive Christianity-like movements, so has new, more stringent interpretation of Christian doctrine emerged. This applies specially to Paul's view of the relationship of Christians to the Law.

Raisanen brings up the work of E. Fuchs in 1949 and his exposition of Romans 5–8.[30] In his exposition, Fuchs proposes that through the death and resurrection of Christ the Law was returned to God after being usurped and stolen by sin. He writes, "Romans 8:2 shows that in Christ 'the law that had been confiscated by sin changed ownership.' The Law has been 'given back to its true master and originator,' and its original significance has been rediscovered."[31] This return allowed the original significance to be revived.

One can now see not abolition of the Law but rebirth. He is presenting the Law of faith as the Law in the Old Testament—as long as it points to Christ. Raisanen points to a different author—F.

---

29. Raisanen and Orton, *Jesus, Paul and Torah*, 50.
30. Raisanen and Orton, *Jesus, Paul and Torah*, 50.
31. Raisanen and Orton, *Jesus, Paul and Torah*, 50.

Hahn, with a somewhat similar view. He defines the Law of the Spirit as that one that comes to pressure the Christian who is now free from under the Law of sin.[32] The intent is not to misunderstand the Spirit as an oppressive agent; rather, as a righteous guide that has suddenly been permitted to take charge guiding the individual in the direction God intends for him. The Christian is now free to follow a path of righteousness.

The teachings of Christ in the Gospel of Matthew reveal another important point. Francois Viljoen explains how Jesus' admonition to obey the Law can be understood from two perspectives. The problem with some of the Pharisees is not that they do not know the Law, but that they interpret it incorrectly.[33] The result is a heavy burden on the people that was never the purpose of the commandments. In other words, there is nothing wrong with the commandment but with those who are manipulating them.

In some ways, the conduct of the teachers of the Law mirrors the rejection of the prophets sent to Israel.[34] Likewise, rejecting the Messiah is rejecting His commandments and instructions (and the only path to salvation, spiritual health, and eternal joy). Christ, in this passage, reaffirms a positive attitude to the Law while admonishing those who misinterpret it.

Christ the Messiah has given a different sort of freedom than mentioned above, implied in the great commission. In Mark 16:15, Christians are commanded to go into all the world and preach the Gospel to all creation. For some, this might not be part of Christian freedom; yet, it allows the individual to express the *words* of freedom. Simultaneously, the individual can, without distorting the core message, use his or her own words to express the newfound freedom in Christ. The main reason why this point is brought up is because the Gospel of Matthew may reveal a stricter view of what it means to fulfil the Great Commission.

Believers are commissioned to make disciples, teaching them to observe, which implies an expectation to put into practice Jesus'

32. Raisanen and Orton, *Jesus, Paul and Torah*, 52.

33. Viljoen, "The Matthean Jesus," 3.

34. Viljoen, "The Matthean Jesus," 9.

Torah.[35] The Sermon on the Mount could be understood as a practical interpretation of the Torah and the commandments. Christ begins by pointing out the need for humility, Moses' greatest trait as explained in Numbers 12:3. The importance of humility is alluded to as a prerequisite for favor in God's eyes all throughout Scripture.

In 2 Chronicles 7:14, humility before God is necessary to obtain forgiveness. In Psalm 25:9, one learns that to grasp God's ways, humility must precede. More importantly, the Prophet Zechariah proclaims the Messiah as "humble and mounted on a donkey" (Zechariah 9:9). Humility must be so important to the Messiah that he chose to teach it first, even before addressing anything else during His sermon.

Next is Solomon's wisdom endowed with practicality in the Sermon on the Mount (Matthew 5). Those who mourn are blessed because they will be comforted by God Himself. People live their entire lives searching for comfort, but none could be greater than God's consolations. Solomon reminds the reader that it is better to go to the house of mourning than to the house of feasting (Ecclesiastes 7:2). Additionally, those who mourn are the object of God's special attention and care (Psalm 9:9, 18:2, 27:4–5, 34:18, 147:3, 86:17, 30:5, 55:22, Joshua 1:9, and Nehemiah 8:10).

Christ refers to yet another aspect of humility—namely, meekness. It seems as if the Messiah is stressing the essential trait of humility as He prepares the ground for understanding. He goes on to describe what characteristics bring blessings. They happen to be the very attributes of God. Christ wants them to live, to be as the living Torah themselves. The peacemakers, the righteous, the persecuted, those insulted—just like God—will inherit all blessings.

Duffield points out that in Matthew, there is a clear call for the church to teach others the instructions of Jesus—and His Torah as delineated on the Sermon on the Mount.[36] The command to preach the Gospel is implied to take second place to a life of

---

35. Duffield, "Difficult Texts," 108.
36. Duffield, "Difficult Texts," 110.

discipleship that emulates God's holiness. Therefore, the call of believers to make disciples is primarily a teaching of the way of life of Christians rather than a campaign for converts. Duffield suggests that Matthew's rendition of the Gospel is one from Torah observant Christians.

On the other hand, there are those who perceive it to be a sin to observe Jewish ceremonial Law as a Christian. Holly Coolman, in her article, "Christological Torah,"[37] refers to Thomas Aquinas as one who controversially makes this claim.[38] She goes on to explain that practicality on this matter reveals that things are not as black and white. One must keep in mind that the people who follow Christ are all part of a community with the same goal.

Consequently, Christians, Jews and the rest of the converts are not called to by any means lose their identity as a people. Rather, it is the diversity and cultural differences within God's family that make the kingdom of God great. For if this were not God's goal, it would not have been revealed to John in his vision. He wrote, "After this I saw a vast crowd, too great to count, from every nation and tribe and people and language, standing in front of the throne and before the Lamb. They were clothed in white robes and held palm branches" (Revelation 7:9, *NLT*). Therefore, Jews do not have to stop being Jews to rest on the assurance of Christ's salvation. For example, they are not necessarily sinning by exercising rituals of purity prescribed by Jewish Law.

Why is any of this important? Simply because, while in the flesh, death has been conquered but sin has not been eradicated. The battle against sin is a daily one—even for the believer. The Holy Spirit thankfully guides and gives the strength to overcome sin. As Christian believers, those who decide to follow observance of Shabbat (or even ritual handwashing before eating bread) are not insulting their maker, but merely attempting to remain pure from sin, if they do not overlook the more important matters of the Law, justice, mercy, and faith (Matthew 23:23). These seemingly unimportant observations can serve as catalysts into a life

37. Coolman, "Christological Torah," Practical Applications.
38. Coolman, "Christological Torah," Practical Applications.

of purity and holiness rather than bringing damnation as Aquinas would propose.[39] In other words, one small act of holiness leads to a greater one, while one small act of mercy conditions the soul for a greater one.

Sin can only be conquered with the help of the Spirit, discipline, and a community of believers. Christians should utilize all these resources to freely love others without discounting any part of the Scriptures. Those who do, fall into heretical ideas that directly oppose the truth of God's Word and misuse their God-given freedom in Christ. Believers are free indeed, but not free to change what is written in Scripture nor to behave in any way opposed to it. The Christian is free to love others by pointing them to Christ and His Word.

39. Coolman, "Christological Torah," Practical Applications.

3

APOSTOLIC VIEW ON FREEDOM

Paul's View on Freedom

PAUL IS THE APOSTLE best known for emphasizing the idea that the righteous shall live by faith. Succinctly, faith in Christ is foundational for believers. For some scholars, Paul is using contradictory theology to the Hebrew Scriptures; yet, upon further consideration, it becomes clear that this is not the case. As mentioned before, the Law was given as a provision to sanctify Israel and to teach the proper way of worshipping God. The Law was never given as a conduit to salvation, but as a path to walk a righteous life in gratitude for God's underserved deliverance.

Nevertheless, it appears that Paul is contradicting Leviticus 18:5, where it says that he who obeys the Law shall live by it.[1] If one obeys the Law, it is because one has faith (belief) in the Law and in the Lawgiver. It might seem that Moses is saying that life comes as a result of submitting to the Law, as many commentators have pointed out, but it could also point to one's path of obedience being the path to follow God's Law—that is, living how it is instructed.

1. Jervis, *Galatians*, 72.

Therefore, Paul is in fact not directly contradicting the Scriptures as some might imagine (at least in relation to Deuteronomy 27:26 and Leviticus 18:5 and, for example, his letter to the Galatians and even in Habakkuk 2:4). Rather, Paul is emphasizing that the righteousness afforded by the Law that gives freedom (Leviticus 26:13) has now been fulfilled by Christ's sacrifice.

The righteousness afforded by the Law of Moses was incomplete due to a person's inability to fulfill all its commandments not because the Law was in and of itself flawed. Instead, it was people's bondage to sin that prevented them from following all requirements of the Law. Regardless of the righteousness attained by either following the Law or by Christ's Atonement, without faith in God, there is no salvation—neither in the Hebrew Bible, nor in the renewed covenant through Jesus Christ. Paul's emphasis is on freedom to love, the perfect law (Romans 6:18, 6:22, 8:21; 2 Corinthians 3:17; Galatians 2:4, 3:14, 5:13; 2 Timothy 2:26; Titus 2:14; and Philemon 1:8).

Ann Jervis explains how other ancient cultures turned to religion and maybe even philosophy to achieve freedom from their fleshly desires, as they knew to be enslaved by them.[2] From her viewpoint, it was clear to the ancient mind who heard Christ's message that freedom in Christ meant freedom from such slavery. She writes, "Pagans turned to religion and philosophy in search of freedom from passions. The challenge was to find a way to be freed from the bondage to the passions and so to achieve god-like peace."[3] It is insightful to see the shift from ancient views that fleshly desires enslaved people, to modern understanding that is far from that perspective. Today, it seems that people are convinced that the more resources or social avenues they can access, the freer they are. For the most part, in the ancient mind, this was not the case as explained above. Therefore, Paul's writings support the Gospel's message.

Paul refers to the Hebrew Scriptures regarding Abraham, who was righteous in God's eyes thanks to his faith, to point out

2. Jervis, *Galatians,* 31.
3. Jervis, *Galatians,* 31.

the expectation of righteousness by faith in the Messiah of Israel.[4] In Hebrews 11, faith is the very thing that the righteous people of the Hebrew Scriptures are commended for. It is essential to know that for all the figures addressed there by Paul, some are walking the path of Torah, and some are not. Nevertheless, they are all grouped in the same category. These individuals were freed from condemnation and ultimate death, thanks to their faith.

Undeniably, Galatians 5:1 is Paul's best succinct stance on Christian liberty: "Stand fast therefore in the liberty by which Christ has made us free, and do not be entangled again by the yoke of bondage." In light of the primary intention of the letter to the Galatians, which is to help those who are attempting to be justified before God by keeping the Law, "the yoke of bondage" could very well have a dual implication. The first possibility could be that the yoke is referring to the oppression of some prescriptions of the Law that might interfere with demonstrating love for a neighbor to the fullest. If someone is drowning in a lake where there is a sign that prohibits swimming, the prohibition in this case should be ignored because love for the victim must simply come first. In this manner, and only in this manner, has the Law of God the potential of being "a yoke of bondage," if it prevents love for one's neighbor.

The second consideration is the primary argument this book rests on—namely, the "yoke of bondage" from which humanity has been freed by Christ, is bondage to sin. Later in the same Epistle, Paul enumerates the works of the flesh, subsequently listed after his admonition to walk in the Spirit of God. He writes, "Walk in the Spirit and you shall not fulfill the lust of the flesh (Galatians 5:16, *NKJV*)." A little further Paul elaborates on the full meaning of the passage, Galatians 5:19–21 proclaims, "Now the works of the flesh are evident, which are: adultery, fornication, uncleanness, lewdness." Therefore, by opening his chapter in this way, Paul has wonderfully included all the ways in which a person is drawn away from the liberty that Christ provides.

---

4. Gager, *Reinventing Paul*, 88.

Peter on Freedom in Christ

Despite difference of opinion between Peter and Paul, the former concedes to Paul's views. This is evident in Galatians 2:6: "And the leaders of the church had nothing to add to what I was preaching. (By the way, their reputation as great leaders made no difference to me, for God has no favorites)." In other words, Paul's message needed no correction. Gary Habermas emphasizes the importance of Paul's encounter with Christ on the road of Damascus.[5] This is key because it corroborated Peter's claim of the bodily resurrection of Christ—another point of agreement. More significantly, Peter's theology on freedom in Christ concentrated on the newfound power to be obedient to Christ (1 Peter 1:2). Peter's tone is stronger yet, comparing Christian freedom to slavery, as it were, to Christ (1 Peter 2:16). This theology parallels the idea that the Hebrew texts' commandments were freeing rather than oppressive.

One way or another, to those who love God—obeying Him through the Law of Moses or through the law of love and grace that Christ quickened by the Spirit of God—is a delight and a joy. Peter is using Hebrew Scriptures' language to establish the relationship between God and His people, one of humility and reverence as seen in Joshua 14:7, 2 Kings 18:12, Psalm 18:1 (among other Scriptural references). He is suggesting that believers in Christ are compared to the righteous individuals of the Scriptures with whom he was familiar.[6]

In his second Epistle, Peter does not fail to present the idea of freedom in Christ as liberation from the yoke of sin, the recurring theme found in the gospels and in Paul's writings (2 Peter 2:19). However, he expounds a step further to a list the character traits that believers are now free to pursue. Among these are, faith, goodness, knowledge, self-control, perseverance, and love. The underlying message is that believers are to become spiritually

---

5. Habermas and Licona, *Case for the Resurrection*, 153.

6. Moo, *2 Peter and Jude*, xxix.

mature[7]—a message also seen in Paul's writings (1 Corinthians 3:2).

The greater possibility of achieving these godly attributes is now permitted because of the liberation from bondage to sin and the empowering of the Holy Spirit. It is important to note how Peter's focus is on purification or sanctification (godliness).[8] He understands that by grace the righteousness of God has been imparted to the believer; thus, now the only appropriate response is to live a life of godliness.

This paradigm is exactly the one found in the Hebrew Scriptures. First, Israel is delivered from the bondage of slavery in Egypt; then, by way of the Law, they are instructed on how to live holy and sanctified lives. Similarly, believers are delivered from the bondage of sin through the renewed covenant ratified by the blood of Christ. Consequently, as Peter points out, the suitable answer is to walk a path of sanctification.

Concerning the original covenant, the conduit for sanctification was the Law. Under the renewed covenant, having been already credited with the righteousness of God, the believer's agent of sanctification is the guidance of the Holy Spirit, who is one in the same with Christ and the Law.

Finally, Peter nearly echoes Paul's words when he says in 1 Peter 2:16 that by being free, the believer should now not use his or her freedom as a cloak of maliciousness, which again leads to servanthood. Moreover, like James, he anticipates trials, to the extent that he understands Christians as being called to suffer—which is not a very popular view today. How could Peter then recognize that people are free yet servants of Christ?

The freedom in question is from slavery to sin unto serving God. Humans were created to be servants of God. The shift occurred upon the first act of sinning that transferred the kingship from God to the evil inclination. Christ's sacrifice rectified the world back to its proper order.

---

7. Moo, *2 Peter and Jude*, xxxv.
8. Moo, *2 Peter and Jude*, xxxv.

James, the Brother of Jesus, on Freedom in Christ

One of the greatest apologetic assets is the conversion of James after Christ's Resurrection. Before the Resurrection (other than his mother, his family, or at least his acquaintances), people were rather skeptical of His ministry (Mark 6:3). Habermas and Licona outline James' transformation upon the Resurrection of his brother.[9] They introduce their logic as follows:

> The Gospels report that Jesus' brothers, including James, were unbelievers during His ministry (Mark 3:21, 31; 6:3-4; John 7:5) . . . 1 Corinthians 15:3-7 lists an appearance of the risen Christ to James . . . James is identified as the leader of the Jerusalem Church . . . his martyrdom is attested by both Christian and non-Christian sources.[10]

A strong point is how the Gospels record the initial unbelief of Jesus' brothers (Mark 3:21, 31, John 7:5).[11] It was not until Acts 15 and the letter of Paul to the Galatians that James is known as the leader of the church in Jerusalem.[12] This confirmation of Christ's brother James as a leader of the church testifies to a life-changing event, namely, the Resurrection (1 Corinthians 15:3-7).

If Christ did not resurrect, what reason could have James then had (after His death) to begin the Christian movement? He, as well as all other disciples, could have moved on with their lives after Christ's death, but this would have certainly not have been the case if they saw Him alive. James assuming leadership of the church in Jerusalem is another collateral evidence for the Resurrection.

James goes on to write a very "matter of fact" letter indicative of the objectivity and down to earth practicality of Jewish mentality. With the same degree of significance as Peter places on grace, James' letter speaks of faith. In James interpretation, faith is the mental attitude of trusting God that cannot be disjointed from action (James 2:26). He points to the Law of liberty, specifically

9. Habermas and Licona, *Case,* 68.

10. Habermas and Licona, *Case,* 68.

11. Habermas and Licona, *Case,* 68.

12. Habermas and Licona, *Case,* 68.

that those Christians living under the grace of God who deny the Law of liberty, deceive themselves. For James, denying the Law of liberty means not abiding by the commandments of Christ. The Law of liberty is analogous to submission to Christ. Paradoxically, submission to Christ brings liberty.[13]

Having a responsibility is typically not perceived as freedom. Yet, James in his Epistle seems to want to convey that God's gift of redemption brings upon oneself the responsibility of morality.[14] This responsibility frees the believers from self-interest allowing him to grow spiritually.[15] He also refers to the Law of Moses as the Law of freedom, as seen in Psalm 19:7.

James and Peter seem to have very similar views regarding the grace of God and freedom in Christ. They are not afraid to bring forth the idea of servanthood to Christ as a sign of true freedom. It is as though the apostles saw submission to God as a privilege. They saw deliverance from sin as the opportunity to finally perform unhindered what was their duty all along, serve God as their king. As it is written in 1 Peter 2:16, *KJV*: "As free, and not using your liberty as a cloak of maliciousness, but as servants of God."

Therefore, it is clear in the apostolic writings that freedom was deliverance from sin unto sanctification and perfect love. Moreover, Paul, James and John have parallel notions of freedom and explain its repercussions in analogous ways. They all express the ancient belief of slavery to sin. From a Jewish viewpoint, no one could liberate them from it but God Himself, in the person of Christ. Their writings not only attest to the teachings of Christ but to their acceptance of His divinity.

Significance of Freedom in Christ

After this in-depth study, the biblical view of freedom in Christ should be rather straight forward. Freedom is to obey and submit

13. Nystrom, *James*, 56.

14. Nystrom, *James*, 72.

15. Nystrom, *James*, 76.

to God and His Word, not to continue to live in bondage to one's desires and passions. In many ways, freedom in Christ meant the same for people at the time of Christ's first coming, as it does today. Yet, as cultures transform, the deceptions of this world evolve alongside becoming more subtle and inconspicuous. Consequently, the significance of freedom in Christ today is slightly distinct than in biblical times.

Significance in Biblical Times

In light of the general understanding of Ancient Near Eastern cultures of the concept to bondage to sin, the true meaning of freedom from it was more readily understood by Christ's contemporaries. This was certainly the case for the religious authorities of the time of Second Temple Judaism. A brief context analysis of the socio-economic and political history of the time might provide greater perspective.

Political, Socio-Economical History
of Second Temple Judaism

Christ was born into a rather complex period in Jewish identity. After the Maccabee's victory,[16] Israel was experiencing a mixture of both freedom and oppression.[17] On the one hand, the Temple was a place that defined Jewish identity, and although Roman governance was present in Judea, the activities taking place there were not hampered. The Jews were free to worship according to the Scriptures.

---

16. The Maccabean Revolt was a Jewish rebellion against the regime of the time, under King Antiochus IV Epiphanes. The Jews primary protest was to the assimilation of Hellenistic culture into Jewish life. They were fighting to uphold their laws and traditions against the overpowering foreign culture. In 167 BCE, the rebellion triumphed. This resulted in the rededication of the temple that is celebrated today and known as the Feast of Lights, or Hannukah. See Johnston, *Ancient Religions*, 186.

17. Bock, *Historical Jesus*, 81.

By 44 BCE, the Roman empire had acquired great power.[18] However, the assassination of Julius Cesar ushered a measure of political distress that ultimately led to the killing also of Antipater, a Macedonian general who had ties to the overseeing of Judea. As a result, Herod, Antipater's son, rose to power. Ironically, the shrewdness of the bloodthirsty Herod led to a period of peace in Judea. Although not a Jew, he allowed worship according to Jewish Law all the while pledging faithfulness to Caesar. Eventually, Rome appointed prefects to ensure governance and revenue. This was the job of Pilate.[19]

Israel was free to carry on with their religious actions, while under constant pressure to remain pure within the constraints of Roman presence. Pilate was fortunate to have the allegiance of the elite of Jewish society, for political reasons, no doubt.[20] At that time, although a combination of both Sadducees and Pharisees comprised the Sanhedrin, the Sadducees appeared to be in control.[21] This was, of course, another source of friction within the religious leadership of Israel. The Sadducees disagreed with many core beliefs of Jewish doctrine with which the Pharisaical movement was convinced.[22]

From a cultural standpoint, Israel was of a considerably large population. Jerusalem alone was estimated to have up to 200,000 inhabitants.[23] The country's major source of revenue was based on fishing and agriculture. Hence, Christ used many references to farming and fishing in His efforts to use language the people would find familiar.

---

18. Bock, *Historical Jesus*, 97.

19. Bock, *Historical Jesus*, 99–100.

20. Bock, *Historical Jesus*, 99–100.

21. Bock, *Historical Jesus*, 99–100.

22. The Pharisees and Sadducees were the Jewish religious leaders in Second Temple Judaism. While the Sadducees embraced the introduction of Hellenistic views into Jewish life, the Pharisees resisted and remained steadfast in upholding the sanctity of Jewish culture. See Choi, *Jewish Leadership*, 85.

23. Bock, *Historical Jesus*, 110.

One must keep in mind that the cultural paradigm of the times was one of honor and shame. This meant that preserving a good reputation was priority. This helps clarify why the disciples were so adamant about Christ not going or even entering the tax collector's house. He would then be not only defiled but lose His reputation and respect from the people.

This information helps with drawing a few conclusions regarding the socio-economic, political, and religious life in which Christ's first coming took place. Israel was free to continue their worship of God without hinderance. Yet, they were forced to pay taxes to Roman authorities by their institution of tax collectors. Although the level of bondage during Roman rule did not compare to, for example, the Babylonian exile, where the people had neither land nor Temple, they were painfully aware of their lack of freedom.

By this time, Israel had already experienced oppression from Persian, Babylonian, and Greek rulership. Their hope for the Messiah was more alive than ever. His coming would once and for all, in their view, free Israel and fulfill the promises to the forefathers. In a rather shortsighted perception of God's power and sovereignty, the forefront of people's minds was focused on deliverance from Roman rule. This would not only symbolize God's favor on the nation, but political freedom for Israel also meant perpetual religious freedom.

Before it accomplished anything else, Christ's self-proclamation of messiahship in Luke 4:18 no doubt stirred up the people's desire for liberation, but also their rejection of Him. Israel was focused on earthly deliverance, while the Messiah had greater plans. His plans targeted the heart of the matter, namely, Israel's rebellion, which was the very thing that had brought them into oppression, originally. Their spiritual separation was in one sense manifest in the division of religious authority between the Pharisees and the Sadducees. The former group was focused on strict Torah observance, while the latter, with a more liberal agenda, rejected the fundamental doctrines of Judaism such as the afterlife, hell, and the bodily resurrection of the dead.[24]

It is no wonder Israel was in state of spiritual confusion. In fact, it was this confusion that contributed to the rejection of Christ.[25] Severino Pancaro asserts that the Gospels, particularly John's, speaks of Christ as not opposed to the Law but in its favor.[26] Pancaro affirms the notion as follows: "The Law is not opposed to Christ (viz., Christ is not opposed to the Law), but speaks in His favor. The Jews, working with a limited (false) understanding of the Law (viz., misunderstanding Christ and the Law itself), are unable to meet the requirements of the Law."[27]

It was the people's ignorance that obscured their understanding. The Messiah upheld that not the smallest part of the Law would be in any way eradicated; yet, Israel was convinced that Christ should be killed for His blasphemy. Moreover, it is the belief of Pancaro that the primary reason that the people rejected their Messiah was ultimately due to their rejection of the Law.[28]

To those who believed, the freedom offered by Christ was priceless. On the natural realm, freedom from Roman rule signified no more death of the innocent, among countless other implications. Moreover, Israel understood that freedom from sin would eventually bring the order of kingship back to God in a kingdom ruled by peace and justice. Infirmity, fear, oppression, slavery, spiritual poverty or otherwise, separation from God, among many afflictions would be things of the past. Eternal reconciliation with God and the institution of His kingdom on earth was the chief significance of the freedom provided in Christ.

---

24. Bock, *Historical Jesus*, 134.
25. Pancaro, *Law in the Fourth Gospel*, 129.
26. Pancaro, *Law in the Fourth Gospel*, 129.
27. Pancaro, *Law in the Fourth Gospel*, 129.
28. Pancaro, *Law in the Fourth Gospel*, 129.

Significance in Modern Times

The last section, in some levels, greatly highlights the significance of freedom in Christ for today's generation. However, with several factors playing a role, more is at stake. For one, the general population has significantly increased, making the number of souls to be reached exponentially greater. It is also debatable if the oppression caused by the bondage to sin is not even greater now than in previous decades. Although human nature remains the same, for those who are without Christ, the way in which sin infiltrates people's lives today is deceptive and instantaneous—particularly with the emergence of television and the internet. Today, very few people do not have access to the internet readily on the palm of their hands.

In postmodernity, having a quick fix for every minor mishap in people's lives could mean that slavery to sin is not so obvious. These days, one with a medical concern is comforted quickly, even in emergency situations. The medical field has developed significantly and is able to perform lifesaving procedures ensuring extension of life to even those with the most sinful lifestyles. One could be deceitfully led to believe that his behavior is not as it were, an affront to God's holiness. Therefore, one might carry on living unrighteous lives bringing upon themselves greater punishment. This is not to say that evil does not also find righteous people; however, it is to affirm Proverbs 19:3. It is written, "The foolishness of a person ruins his way, and his heart rages against the Lord." Amidst all, freedom in Christ means to suddenly be aware of the small voice of God that gently reminds of the subtle oppressive nature of all sinful behavior.

It is important to note that believers serving God as well as those who are servants of the other kingdom, both live and run, sort of speak, in the same rat race. The key is that the servants of God glorify and usher His kingdom by their actions while others glorify the kingdom of darkness. Additionally, freedom in Christ gives the believer the peace of letting go of all that is tangible with the assurance that nothing can compare to what God has in store in the world to come for those who love Him. If this statement seems farfetched, it might be helpful to point out that such peace is ultimately true in a believer's life, but it might take a long journey. Coming to grips with reality and acceptance of one's fate is a process equally difficult for Christ's followers as it is for everyone else. The humanity in people remains.

The directions given by Christ and His disciples uphold the legal code of the Mosaic Law and its timeless principles.[29] Depending on what part of the world where one lives today, it is likely that his circumstances are not as that of those who lived under Roman rule. Yet, for those who are living in countries of oppression and persecution, they can have the hope and peace offered by Christ's freedom. Lioy explains that believers have the freedom to live according to a higher principle than that of sin.[30] So, does this not mean that one does concern himself with addictions or repeated transgressions at all? Hardly.

The believer is subject to the influence of his evil inclination that remains even in the presence of the Holy Spirit. However, because of His presence, it is possible to reject such enticements by the newly acquired power (1 John 4:4). In his first letter, John explains, "You, little children, are from God and have overcome them, because greater is He who is in you than he who is in the world."

Today, more than ever, people should be encouraged to think critically about their beliefs. Contrary to popular belief, this is what the Bible invites people to do (Isaiah 1:18, 1 Thessalonians 5:21). It is critical in our day to stop and self-examine, frequently. This is true for God's children and it true for those of the world.

If people were to take the time to self-examine and take a break from their fast-paced routines, they would give themselves the opportunity to discover the delusions of the contemporary views of postmodernity. Even upon superficial examination, such views prove to be unsound— both theoretically and practically. The movements that embrace individualism and relativism in

29. Lioy, *Jesus as Torah*, chapter 2.
30. Lioy, *Jesus as Torah*, chapter 2.

many ways have proven to violate the basic laws of logic by defying not just reason but pragmatism. In the following chapter, Postmodernism will be explored in some depth to gain a better understanding of the challenges that evangelists face at reaching the world.

4

Ideology of the Modern World

Postmodernism?

This chapter sets the backdrop for the spiritual and social battlefield in which committed Christian find themselves, at the moment. The idealism of the Postmodern worldview is the most widespread at least in the West, although with the globalization of internet accessibility, the world's morality it is not easily distinguishable any longer. It is important to understand that *today's age* is not as new as some might suppose. Rather, the modernism period ended its stage some generations ago. In fact, some might even argue that postmodernity is already a thing of the past and now an even greater progressive position prevails.

Tyson E. Lewis writes, "The task of philosophy is thus to capture the dying old world before it fades away. Perhaps we are now in a similar situation with Postmodernism, which has become a boring, contradictory, and dying cliché. In this sense, Postmodernism, like the work of art in the age of mechanical reproduction, is losing its aura and becoming a ruin."[1] It is difficult to define these terms as one attempts to give justice to those oblivious of

---

1. Lewis, "Studying Postmodernism," 1342–43.

their own situation. Yet, this is but another undesirable ramification of their perspective. In effect, if those overcome by this world would but for a moment be made aware of their state of unreason, one might suspect an immediate reaction of shock and incredulity.

As previously mentioned, the decisive turn into Postmodernism can be traced as far back as to the Enlightenment Era.[2] It was then that the speedy development of science in many ways came in at odds with those of a theological worldview.[3] Undoubtedly, this trend is still very much alive today, but formerly secularism was driven by science and discoveries, which paved the way for modern thought. This principle has exponentially expanded in recent decades.

L. Russ Bush parallels the views of society before and after modernity. He divides the comparison between two views: an earlier and a modern one. Whereas the modern one is characterized by a belief in natural evolution, the survival of the fittest depicts humankind as the pinnacle of biological evolution. The earlier view perceived humanity as divinity created in a world where the survival is of the faithful and mankind is defined by his spiritual failure.[4]

The three aspects mentioned above regarding people's understanding are necessary to make the point. Regarding nature for example, a previous view was that humans were created (and not evolved) from some lower form of life. Pertaining history, the new view ascribes to the survival of the fittest as opposed to the survival of the faithful. Finally, regarding humankind, the new view believes in intrinsic spiritual progress in contrast to an acknowledgment of failure and the need for God.[5] In other words, a total paradigm reversal has occurred.

As mentioned before, some even go as far as to say that Postmodernism had already ended at the turn of the century.[6] Yet, it

2. Bush, *Advancement*, 7.

3. Bush, *Advancement*, 8.

4. Bush, *Advancement*, 15.

5. Bush, *Advancement*, 15.

6. McHale, *Cambridge Introduction*, 171.

seems to endure beyond its very defining moment at the end of the Cold War in 1991, and it appears that it has come to stay. It is therefore significant.[7] It would be wise to start at the beginning, however. The global period of ongoing "Cold" war that began in 1947 seems to have generated such a cultural impact that revolutionized, yet again, and ushered in another wave of liberal culture.[8] This yet again, new cultural enlightenment, entices one to live for the moment, for tomorrow the only surety is that of death. This then, in conjunction with the technological advances of the past fifty years, have produced a way of life that oddly allows very little time to think.

In defining Modernism, it might be helpful to understanding its successor. Innovation and advancement are at the heart of the modern mind, in and of itself not intrinsically evil, but is the cost paid for such progress worth its price? Brian McHale explains that a self-destructive modernist view necessarily calls for its "new and improved" inheritor.[9] He writes, "Eventually, this relentless logic of superseding oneself requires that modernism itself becomes obsolete, necessitating a successor—Postmodernism."[10] As in a state of perennial inebriation, in hopes of escape the here and now, for the Postmodern, one must always be looking into what is to come—the greatest thief of what has already arrived. This is but one of the most tragic prices to pay for this mindset.

Modernity is in some ways a manifestation of the paradox between innovation and destruction. The more the world develops longevity schemes, it also further develops weapons of mass destruction. What is new and improved in a positive aspect is also new and improved in the negative. The greatest danger seems to be in the implication of the concept that new is always better. Without sliding down the slippery slope of defining good and evil, the assumption regarding what is better is not that which produces the

---

7. McHale, Cambridge Introduction, 1.

8. McHale, Cambridge Introduction, 1.

9. McHale, Cambridge Introduction, 4.

10. McHale, Cambridge Introduction, 4.

highest monetary profit. Rather, it is that which benefits society the most as an interconnected unit.

This is exemplified—although to the extreme—in the words of Caiaphas at the so-called trial of Christ. Unbeknownst to him, he prophesied: "Nor do you understand that it is better for you that one man should die for the people, not that the whole nation should perish" (John 11:50, *ESV*). Caiaphas was affirming the concept that God accepts atonement for sin through the sacrifice of the righteous. In other words, the benefit of society is placed over the rights and benefit of one individual.

This is what, from a biblical viewpoint, means to do good and usher genuine progress. The implication of "the new is always better mentality" is that maybe consciously or most often unconsciously, one believes that the new must always be better. This subtly suggests that those who created the new are in some ways "better" and wiser than the creators of the old.

This notion could not be further from the truth. Erroneously, it creates a sense of unsubstantiated superiority and pride that undermines the contributions of those who paved the way for the invention to even be possible. This breeds all sorts of problems between generations and families. The home being the very unit that seems to be the enemies' primary target. Once the home institution has been compromised, the enemy more than has the upper hand. Herein lies the other paramount effect of the Postmodern mentality.

It is obvious that the breakup of the family is the gravest consequence of postmodernist ideologies. Yet, if society chooses to accept progress as inevitable, then people are simply rejecting reason. Those of this worldview belong to a society that does not believe the reasons why age-old metanarratives were accepted and embraced. They fail to accept how traditional understanding of the world generates the "best" possible outcome for society.

To those who ask about their right to do as they please, about the infringement of the first amendment, one could propose the following paradoxical premise. The majority who support the idea of progress along with expressions of personal freedom, are often working under the premise of good deeds, and at times in the name of love. Few people would deny this statement. For example, those who claim to make the world a better place by providing better technology, better kitchen appliances, better home entertainment, aim to make life easier and more enjoyable. This is, to an extent, true. Yet, better kitchen appliances are also more expensive, forcing the family to work harder and longer to acquire them. In this additional effort, the family is drawn apart. As a result of the extra efforts, they are seldom home long enough to enjoy the very thing that was supposed to draw them together.

Based on this basic example (and countless others), one could say it is true that the greater the "progress," the higher the risk to the family.[11] Some might bring forth an important point—that is, that the creator of that which is new, had the right intention, but it was the user who perverted the purpose of the creation. If this is completely true, which is at least possible, then the product should have been made available—not only making life easier, but also easy to acquire and affordable. Thus, the best interest of society is truly the intention of the creator. If, on the other hand, the profit made by the advancement is, in fact, the driving force, that is not a sign of true love for others but love of self.

Some might ask, "Are not all things that are new and improved necessarily more expensive? Does this concept not foment a sense of healthy ambition? Is it not the profit of one's work that which motivates creativity?" The answer is "yes" and "no." One can create a new washing machine less expensive to produce and to buy. One also can charge more than the previous washing machine without charging so much more that is price prohibitive for the average family to purchase. Creativity is only good when it benefits people

---

11. In his book, *Sacro-Egoism: The Rise of Religious Individualism in the West*, John S. Knox sets out to dissect one of the latest trends. That is, the shift of western culture to individualism, subjectivation, and autonomization from a communal oriented mindset. This transition is no doubt, at least partially, a result of current societal progress. The ability of an individual to more greatly thrive without the support of family or community foments, in some ways, a form of toxic individualism that can be harmful for family and community alike, but specially for the individual. See Knox, *Sacro-Egoism*, 124, 128–29.

truly, and when it benefits society. As a result of an evil kind of creativity, society breaks apart, and consequently the world itself. Although progress might temporarily bring ease and comfort, if it was not brought forth in love of anyone except of him who makes a profit, then, instead of progress, it is ultimately just digression.

The Irrationality of Postmodernism

The principle of Postmodernism has infiltrated all aspects of life. This is in no way to affirm that being one who understands his rights and fosters creativity and self-expression is somehow society's antagonist. Rather, it is to insist that if the result of their actions is detrimental to the world, then those actions have no right to fall within the category of "love acts." Those who insist on that illusion are simply self-deceived. They have fallen away from that which Christians call the truth.

As many authors have pointed out, one of the greatest defining characteristics of Postmodernists is their derision not only for what is depicted as truth, but their adamant hostility against it being defined by someone else whom they encounter. This concept in and of itself is self-refuting for obvious reasons. One author explains that the very claim—"All is relative and there are no such thing as ineffable truths"—constitutes a truth claim—unless, of course, it is relative in which case the speaker has no point whatsoever.[12] By a simple rule of reason, this statement must necessarily be false.

An argument from silence has proven ineffective for both believers and non-believers in making their point. To affirm that atheism or theism are true, just because there is a possibility they could be, establishes a rather weak argument. L. Russ Bush's statement carries considerable weight in defense of a theistic worldview. He asserts that what modern scientists believe is even more extraordinary than theism itself.[13] The idea of the alleged big bang

---

12. Niall et al., Dictionary of Postmodernism, 191.

13. Bush, *Advancement*, 29.

explosion, that after a nearly infinite and random set of interactions emanates the origin of creation, seems to require greater faith in such events generating the present complexity of life than the level of faith necessary to believe in a rational powerful being fashioning it all.[14] Furthermore, believing such a theory only for the sake of not giving in to the theistic defender seems neither healthy nor rational.

It might surprise many that the scientific quickening of the Enlightenment Era found its spark in Christianity itself.[15] Many universities and hospitals were founded and are named after people of faith. The foundations of modern science were laid by those who understood that human's epistemological access is only possible through the existence of a God who has made it so. Otherwise, if the mind, what believers believe to be the soul, is only a result of natural processes, it cannot be objective about what it judges.[16]

For this reason (and others), despite the Postmodern's belief that there are no objective unchangeable truths, they find themselves forced to base their worldview on assumptions that necessarily become their truth claims. For the Postmodern individual, freedom as an extreme definition is incompatible with reality. Francis Schaeffer writes, "The freedom that was being sought was an absolute freedom with no limitations. There is no God . . . at the same time, he feels the damnation of being in the machine. This is the tension of the modern man."[17] One can clearly see the internal contradiction in a world made of such concepts.

Many assumptions are made by those of a naturalist viewpoint; yet, some more than others prove themselves beyond irrational. For example, a naturalist believes by implication, that living organisms originated from non-living matter.[18] Upon but a brief observation of nature, one can clearly see that all matter can and

14. Bush, *Advancement*, 29.

15. Bush, *Advancement*, 19.

16. Bush, *Advancement*, 61.

17. Schaeffer, *Escape from Reason*, 75.

18. Bush, *Advancement*, 68.

only produces more of itself. Therefore, nothingness, emptiness and chaos can only give rise to more of the same. The obvious contingency of all creation has been blatantly ignored.

Postmodernists, therefore, are those who without reason chose to live in a state of incredulity towards all meta-narratives of the "past."[19] Opposition to the truth of a Creator and the production of manmade set of values and ideologies is nothing more than the branches' rebellion against the tree.[20] The branches do so for the sake of claiming their right to be free to believe and think on their own. Yet, in doing so, they abandon all hope and reason. They abandon their own humanity. This can be compared to the limbs of a person who have rebelled against him. They claim they can survive on their own without the need of the body. However, those limbs, if severed from the man, being no longer part of him, not only die, but also lose their role. In the same way, if man separates from the truth of God to create His own truths, he has essentially redefined himself—thereby renouncing his humanity.

This is what C. S. Lewis referred to in his famous work, *The Abolition of Man*.[21] Lewis writes, "We make men without chests and expect of them virtue and enterprise."[22] That is to say, to deny reason is to deny humanity itself. To fight against the existence of absolute truths is more self-destructive than kicking against the bricks.

There are healthier and more mature ways to deal with the human desire of independence and even contempt against authority. Postmodernism cannot be embraced because it contradicts, misrepresents, and denies at least some aspects of reality.[23] Furthermore, it has proven to be self-refuting, thereby designating itself unenforceable. Those who chose to hold to irrationality for the sake of disagreement, are not headed for progress but for destruction.

19. Niall et al., Dictionary of Postmodernism, 49.

20. Lewis, *Abolition of Man*, 44.

21. Lewis, *Abolition of Man*, 26.

22. Lewis, *Abolition of Man*, 26.

23. Bush, *Advancement*, 85.

Understanding Their Position

What if those with a theistic viewpoint were to ask themselves these questions: "How is it possible that considering the obvious irrationality intrinsic to Postmodernism, that some still chose to stand by it? What force could be strong enough to imprison a person in such a manner that he has abandoned all reason?" One is forced to resort to pain and suffering.

Unquestionably, many who refuse to give up irrationality do so simply not to give the opposing party the triumph, as it were. This might, in fact, be the most irrational and sad fact of all. Yet, for most, the issue is a more complicated one. Those who deny the reality of absolute truth, the existence of God being of primary importance, appear to not have found a healthy way to embrace the pain and suffering the world experiences daily. In other words, they cannot conceive that a loving God, who is actively involved in His creation permits such horrors. They cannot conceive of a purpose for the suffering.

For them, an argument from absence does not satisfy. That is to say that there is not gratuitous evil, and that God has a purpose for it all. Yet, if humanity is not able to conceive it, this is not to imply that is not possible. This argument from silence simply does not answer some people's yearning for justice. Still, who can blame them? They were after all made in the image of a God of justice.

This is the reality that Christians must assist people in understanding, especially those who do not know how to deal with their pain. It is critical to understand that for those who deny God because of the existence of evil, there is no other response but to outright deny the possibility of a benevolent being who permits it. Unquestionably, for some, there will never be a strong enough argument to convince of a good that would justify evil. However, for others, it takes only greater understanding of but a few unanswered questions to free them from the confinement of the Postmodern worldview.

The implications of such levels of disapproval of the God of the Christians and Jews are numerous. For those individuals, atheism is not only a plausible answer but a necessity. Secularization is therefore a direct result of a sort of disenchantment of their hopes and aspirations.[24] This universal experience, Callum Brown contends, is the greatest cultural transition in Western society.[25] He writes, "We need to get beyond thinking of atheism as solely concerning Nietzsche and the "new atheists" in philosophical and controversialist modes . . . We need the atheists' appreciation of the social history of atheism, in all its flourishing diversity."[26] However, as mentioned before, the abandonment of the concept of a world founded and governed by God, inevitably ushers in an age of undesirable self-assertion and individualism.

Again, in and of themselves, these desires are not evil, but when they become an afront to the welfare of society, evil emerges. One could then conclude that the universality and prevalence of secularism is at least in some ways a result of two major desires. They are the human inclination to defy authority and their undying longing for a suitable explanation for the evil in the world.

Richard Wolin wrote a work entitled, *The Seduction of Unreason*.[27] In it, he presents yet another ramification. He refers to the writings of Friedrich Nietzsche who made the famous assertion: "Truth is a kind of error without which a certain species of life could not live."[28] Some would wonder what sort of response the author of this assertion would give when asked to evaluate the authenticity of the statement itself. The point Wolin is trying to make is that unreason is a kind of seduction that afflicts even great thinking minds. This seduction is the ultimate expression of asserting one's desire to designate what is truth.

Put another way, if God is in fact the source of all truth, then those embracing this seduction are merely embracing the oldest deception in the history of mankind. Namely, they wanting to be like God. Unfortunately, the power of this deception is such

24. Brown, "Necessity of Atheism," 452.
25. Brown, "Necessity of Atheism," 452.
26. Brown, "Necessity of Atheism," 456.
27. Wolin, Seduction of Unreason, 33.
28. Wolin, Seduction of Unreason, 33.

that those overcome by it are oblivious to its artful manipulation. Whether one is seduced by a romantic partner or an ideology, too often only those who are on the outside can clearly see. Hence, Nietzsche gives the typical response of someone who fails to plainly comprehend his own state of affairs. He charges with having succumbed to seduction those who do believe in absolute truths.[29] He is, in fact, the one in denial.

There may be a plethora of manifestations of the desire to rebel. Of them, only a couple were mentioned. Some, more understandable than others. However, they all fall under the same category. Such is the inherent rebellious nature of the human heart and its undying desire to be not merely like God, but to be God. What is so bad after all about wanting to be like Him who made humans? In the end, for those who believe God to be their father, are not they called to be like God? Just, merciful, holy. This is a fair question. The children of God are called to be *like* God. They are not called to *be* God.

Christian Freedom and Secular Freedom

Secular freedom is easily identifiable. Parents and grandparents speak about it all the time to their children. One must strive to accomplish a good education. With it, financial freedom comes, and life is easy. Unfortunately, those who have reached the top of that mountain discover a rather hollow victory. This is not to undermine all the benefits of hard work and education, by no means. Still, even the Bible maintains that money answers everything (Ecclesiastes 10:19). However, since what Solomon is addressing in this verse are the things that money can afford, he must necessarily be referring to earthly things. No one would presume that money can buy spiritual wealth. There is no currency for spiritual affluence, other than obedience to the Word of God and acts of kindness, of course. For this reason, Christ said in Mark 12:17, *BSB*: "Give to Caesar what is Caesar's and what is God's to God."

29. Wolin, Seduction of Unreason, 35.

So, a question arises, could secular freedom afford the peace spiritual beings, humans in this case, so desperately need? If not, why? Secular freedom, having the choice of staying at a 5-star hotel as easily as staying at a two-star hotel for example, produces ease and enjoyment in life, but this does not equal true freedom. How so? If the peace of the individual who suddenly loses the financial power to live this lifestyle is extinguished, this is a clear indication that he was in fact not free from the cares of this world. Being imprisoned by at least something in and of itself abrogates true freedom. This person is bound to his life in such a way that losing any aspect of it can rock him to his core. Therefore, not only is he a slave to whatever activity that produces the resources to live lavishly, in the case of loss, his identity also perishes.

There are many nuances of this enslavement, cultural, social, and even religious. Culture's influence on one's image can be quite gripping. To a degree, no one is completely exempt. Except for those communities that have chosen to live completely isolated from society, lifestyle of which the Bible disapproves. Christians are called to be in the world but be not of the world. Only in this way they can be the light of the world. New fashion trends, social paradigms, religious activities constantly fluctuate in such a rapid dynamic that those who are concerned with keeping up, fall victim to the need of maintaining their income stream at all costs. It is there that the opposite of freedom manifests itself.

Ironically, it can be argued that in some measure, those with a secular worldview are in fact aware of their lack of freedom, even those who endorse nihilism, such as Frederick Nietzsche. He writes, "The only way we can overcome our servitude is by knowing we are not free."[30] This recognition by an atheist is the perfect example of grasping what appears to be a profound state of despair in someone without the freedom of Christ. Frederick Nietzsche, a renown philosopher, composer and even poet,[31] would certainly have enjoyed the luxuries of life. At least at one point in his life, if not all his life, he had access to the freedoms this world has to offer.

30. Wolin, Seduction of Unreason, 85.
31. Wolin, Seduction of Unreason, 33.

Yet, he finds himself recognizing that he is nothing more than in a state to servitude. If he in fact "had it all," as it were, one could read his statement as coming from someone not truly at peace although he possesses the freedom of this world.

Christian freedom is altogether different. It is important to point out that Christians also see themselves as servants, but of God (Psalm 113:1, 1 Peter 2:16). Paradoxically, this servitude is one that results in freedom. In order to understand this idea of inescapable servitude one must go back to the account of the creation. One must perceive what the purpose of humanity was then and still is.

Upon understanding the nature of a tree, for example, one can quickly arrive at least at two conclusions. First, one would realize its possible purposes, and equally important, its inability of being anything other than what it is. A tree cannot be used for the purpose of cutting a piece of metal, nor does it have the ability to turn into something that would. Similarly, a human being created for the purpose for serving, does not possess in himself the ability of changing into something that would not.

In Genesis, the Lord instructs Adam to have dominion over the creation and subdue it (Genesis 1:28, *ESV*). He also instructs them to be fruitful and multiply. He is instructing Adam to live and to produce more life. Later in the account of Cain and Abel, the word, עֹבֵד (*obed*), literally "servant" of the ground is used when describing Cain's occupation. This teaches that the act of subduing, working the earth, the act of carrying on with God's intention for man was one of servitude. Such servitude has a positive undertone, not a negative one. The Scriptures are clear. Only those who obey God's commandments are truly free (Psalm 119:45). In conclusion, man was created to serve, and he is not capable of freeing himself from this role. Both serve, but those who belong to God serve Him while those who belong to the other kingdom nevertheless still serve.

Therefore, it appears that the issue of true freedom is directly related to the object of the service and not to the service itself. In other words, humans were made to serve so serve they shall.

Yet, what affords them freedom is whom they serve. If they serve themselves, they are in fact enslaved. Alternatively, if their service is to God, then and only then are they truly free. Some might ask if this is so, then it should be evident to all people. What is the indication that one is serving the wrong kingdom? The answer has already been mentioned above. The servants of the earthly kingdom do not have true peace.

5

IMPLEMENTING FREEDOM IN CHRIST
AS AN APOLOGETIC TOOL

THUS FAR, THERE HAS been an attempt in dispelling any misunderstandings of what Christian freedom is, truly. This clarification is as crucial for the believer as much as it is for the non-believer. For the disciple of Christ, it accomplishes two primary objectives. First, it is used for the sake of a biblically adherent walk with God. Second, it is for the message that is transmitted to those meant to be reached as brought forth in the great commission of Christ. For evangelistic purposes, it is in defense of God's reputation and for the support in an individual's sanctification, that understanding freedom in Christ is vital. Still, one must not forget the importance of a godly person's exercise of balance in all aspects of his life.

It could be argued that freedom in Christ is equally important for the non-believer. While one (in some cases) is unaware of the subtle masked subjugation of the world, in many cases, those under earthly servitude are quite clear and weary in their situation. For some, their predicament is evident and plain; for others, it expresses itself in ways that one is not able of precisely identifying. So, people drift into a state of limbo where they are neither truly happy and at peace, nor are they completely miserable. They have simply settled for a life of discontent. It ought not be this way, for Christ came to give life, and that more abundantly.

The first question to ask perhaps is regarding the current approaches that the church is employing in the field of apologetics. This subject, as a defense of faith in Christ, certainly takes many faces, but above all, it must be comprehensive. For those who believe, these are issues of life and death. A successful apologist must therefore use all means available to him to get the message across without using manipulation, patronizing arguments, or condescending statements. Above all, he should be able to speak the truth about sections of the Word of God and about realities of this world that are not so easily explained and accepted. These things require strength, conviction, and patience.

Willem Van Vlastuin succinctly describes the three main modern schools of thought in apologetics.[1] The first approach draws on an encounter with God, His direct revelation, and human reason via natural theology.[2] The second attempt at the modern defense of the Christian faith is a combination of both Classical Apologetics and Evidentialism. Finally, Presuppositionalism and Reformed Apologetics constitute the last major category.[3] The purpose of this work is not to place its argument under any of these categories. Rather, it is to implement freedom in Christ into each of the three.

The implications of suggesting a one-size-fits-all complementary apologetics would undermine their distinct relevance and efficacy. This idea would at least partially insinuate that the different branches of apologetics on their own cannot stand. Nothing could be further from the truth. Each approach is designed to speak of a different manifestation of God's revelation—and to everyone's unique intellect. Yet, there is no reason not to derive benefit from applying freedom in Christ into each school of thought.

---

1. Vlastuin, "Complementary Apologetics," 1–9.
2. Vlastuin, "Complementary Apologetics," Intro.
3. Vlastuin, "Complementary Apologetics," Intro.

Freedom in Christ and Classical Apologetics

The significance of reason and facts in classical apologetics sets the groundwork for subsequent developments. In this facet of defense, the most basic arguments are built. In Classical apologetics (for the most part), the basis is not Scriptural truths, in as much as they do not always rest on human reason. Classical apologists argue that mere observation of the world with emphasis on human reason is sufficient proof for the necessity of God. Arguments such as those derived from the laws of logic bring forth a strong case for a reasonable theistic worldview. Justin Martyr, Anselm of Canterbury, and Thomas Aquinas are relevant figures in this school of thought.[4] Although some pioneers of classical apologetics affirm that philosophy alone is not sufficient to justify the Christian faith, philosophy has served as foundational for many subsequent works of classical apologetics.[5] The basis of philosophy being reason itself.

Natural theology is another significant area of this field. The uniformity of nature and its consistency serve as supporting evidence to logic and human reason. Arguments such as the teleological and ontological ones are foundational to later works. Ancient Christian thinkers, by affirming the unbreakable relationship between faith and reason, in some ways have introduced a model that argues for the necessary rational relationship between freedom in Christ and obedience to God. If in fact humans were created to be servants of God and by implication, of each other, such service is the fulfilment of obedience that results in freedom.

The argument at present is a combination of teleological and an overall classical use of reason. The teleological argument, put succinctly, speaks to the requirement of an intelligent Creator. The Creator has made a world in which everything has a purpose and nothing in it was created frivolously. This concept comes in stark contrast with the atheist's view of nihilism. Human existence itself has the end of servitude as does the rest of the creation. The

4. Edgar and Oliphint, *Christian Apologetics,* 35, 365, 395.
5. Edgar and Oliphint, *Christian Apologetics,* 396.

contingency of the world speaks to this notion. The food chain defines nature's idea of servitude. All components of nature in their existence as sustenance for other species serve with the end of maintaining and producing more life. To this end, they glorify their Creator who is the ultimate source of it.

With this assumption in mind, it is important to consider how humans view the creation as truly free. Many have heard at some point others express their desire to be like the birds of the sky or like the fish in the sea. They are wishing for what they understand to be their ideal state of freedom. Fish and birds are in fact free from human responsibilities such as paying bills and being on time at work. Yet, animals in their teleological nature have also reproductive responsibilities and service duties to the rest of the creation. To them, this is all instinctive and even joyful to the extent that humans clearly perceive them as free. On the other hand, people do not seem to see themselves in the same light. Instead, their service to the creation, to God and each other is more of a burden. This ought not to be.

If, in fact, adhering to God' commandments bring freedom (like it so obviously does for the rest of creation), reason affirms that this truth also applies to humanity. Birds sing upon seeing the sun rise. Those same birds are a link in the food chain. They do not know when they will die or from where will their next meal come; yet, they see themselves as free to bring more life into the world and sing in gratitude for another day. Their servitude does not hinder their freedom.

Following this line of reasoning, with the teleological purpose of the creation of which humans are its pinnacle, humans can logically conclude that their understanding of freedom is reverse to the order of nature. Therefore, only those with a theological worldview have the right to claim true freedom. The fish are free even though they are contingent upon the rest of the creation and the creation is contingent upon them. Birds are free even though they are servants to their offspring and to the creatures to whom they serve as sustenance. Birds are free even if they are completely dependent on external provision for all their needs. In the same way, humans are free when they fulfill all their responsibilities mandated by God with the purpose with which He created them.

Humans feel that true freedom is simply permission to do as they please. Humanity sees freedom as having the right to disregard their duty and role in the creation. This, however, is contrary to life and due to human fallen nature. How then can someone who is an intrinsic part of nature believe himself to be above it? Although it is undeniable that humans are the pinnacle of the creation, they too are contingent upon it and consequently accountable to it. Someone who understands this concept, yet still believes that he is above the world from which he depends—simply because he has been endowed with greater understanding—proves his lack thereof (if not of absurdity). In this manner, the arguments used in classical apologetics support the essential nature of freedom in Christ. More importantly, it is this understanding of freedom that becomes so valuable to those who embrace it.

Reformed Apologetics

John Calvin's work has served as the canvas for further development in the camp of Reformed Apologetics. For Calvinists, employing reason is only secondary to people's innate sense of divinity.[6] Arguments from nature are good but almost unnecessary because they are simply too obvious. Upon observing nature, God's existence is undeniable. From the viewpoint of natural theology, humans have been given such a powerful witness of God's existence that they are without excuse. Therefore, classical apologetics in some ways would imply that reason alone could be the conduit to encountering God. Reformed apologists deny this possibility without disregarding reason's role in apologetics. In other words, reason has its place, but it is limited.

It is not lack of reasoning abilities that prevents man from ascertaining the truth of God but his fallen nature. Sin is the dark cloud through which sinners cannot see the Son. Furthermore,

---

6. Edgar and Oliphint, *Christian Apologetics*, Vol. 2, 40.

since faith is paramount, arguments dependent on reason are unsuccessful at introducing the required faith. This God Himself must give to those in need. God must be directly involved and only He can open the eyes of the blind. The Reformers are not saying that reason does not help in understanding matters of knowing of God. Instead, they assert that the primary experience with Him must take place via the testimony of the Holy Spirit.[7]

How does any of this relate to freedom in Christ? In other words, in what ways does the Holy Spirit testify of freedom in Christ in connection with obedience to God? According to Christianity, endowment with the Holy Spirit has been provided to humanity thanks to Christ's atoning work. Therefore, all revelation, teaching, understanding, and wisdom comes by way of the Spirit of God. The Spirit of God teaches that which Christ did not have the chance to before His return to the Father. This same Spirit is the transformer and molder of the new man in Christ.

Of those who have had the privilege of meeting God, as explained in Christian terms, similar descriptions are given. They experience a sudden and drastic change in personality and demeanor. They are those who (overnight in some cases) have changed their lifestyles from obviously being lost in this world to models of godliness and respect. Such individuals are characterized by two defining traits. They are a deep sense of humility and an inherent attitude of servitude. Thus, it is evident in the life of those who have been gifted with Christ's freedom that such freedom, while it yet remains, is manifested in service to humanity.

Anselm's work in *Discourse on the Existence of God*, is exemplary of Presuppositionalism and Revelational Apologetics, with its defining term of "Reformed Apologetics." In it, he distinguishes in simple terms the basis of human understanding of the world from a theological viewpoint. He states, "For I cannot seek thee, except thou teach me, nor find thee, except thou reveal thyself . . . Unless I believed, I should not understand."[8] Therefore, the crucial question for the apologist, from a Reformed perspective,

---

7. Edgar and Oliphint, *Christian Apologetics*, Vol. 2, 41.

8. Edgar and Oliphint, *Christian Apologetics*, Vol. 1, 373.

seems not to be to explain the necessary existence of an unchanging and eternal Creator. Rather, the point is to assist the person in accepting God as the Creator and redeemer as the basis of his understanding of reality.

It is not until that moment that the other aspects of reality—both seen and unseen—become apparent. It is not until then that everything makes sense. The first treasure to be discovered is in many ways liberating. There is a certain freedom in clear understanding. Then, the Spirit of God imparts the freeing desire to serve. This service is not taxing. This service is not in toil and pain. This service is the original intention for the human creation. It liberates the mind, body, and soul from servitude with wrong motives and intentions.

Presuppositionalism

This school of thought assumes a priori that the Bible is true. This statement alone is controversial enough. In addressing the challenges that apologists face regarding Postmodernism, it is the most effective. The concepts of relativism and naturalism that define a Postmodern worldview are best handled through the employment of a presuppositionalistic response.[9] Presuppositionalists are not implying to have blind faith on a book filled with nonsense. Rather, they propose that a biblically theistic worldview is in fact the highest level of rationality.[10]

The work of Cornelius Van Til is relevant in this arena. In *The Defense of the Faith*, he explains how the approach to this type of reasoning is indirect rather than direct.[11] This is to say that the disagreement between theist and atheist is impossible to solve on direct analysis of the facts of nature, for example. Rather, these matters indirectly depend on who defines the facts of natural law,

---

9. Dulles, *History of Apologetics*, 357.

10. Dulles, *History of Apologetics*, 358.

11. Edgar and Oliphint, *Christian Apologetics*, Vol. 2, 460.

either theist, or atheist.[12] For those who assume biblical inherency, the creation with all its laws is in direct opposition to the understanding of a naturalistic mindset. Therefore, it is the job of the apologist in this school of thought to present a biblical worldview as the most rational of all options.

In the same work, Van Til asserts that indeed the natural man is aware of his created nature. He is aware of his obligation to God in the form of both responsibilities and grateful service.[13] However, Val Till continues, the natural man suppresses this awareness. So, it is the objective of the presuppositionalist to counteract the suppression.[14]

This is in many ways, easily accomplished and, in some ways rather complex. This brings the matter of the controversy of biblical inherency to center stage. The soundness of biblical teachings is undeniable, even for the atheist. From the book of Proverbs and Ecclesiastes alone, there are several layers of wisdom and instruction for all people. Few scholars would disagree.

Yet, skeptics who agree with this statement do not attribute the same level of trustworthiness to the other portions of Scripture. Skeptics are unable to accept that Noah had (at one point) all land animals on his ark. Bible critics reject that Jonah was in the belly of a fish for three days, or that Christ exponentially multiplied a few pieces of bread and fish on two separate occasions. This is particularly troublesome to the modern mind.

Incredible stories circulate on the news throughout the world daily. Stories of incredible feats of strength, like women lifting cars with their hands from babies to save their lives after a car accident. Many such unbelievable stories are in fact true, like the one that quickly was made into a book and a movie, *The Life of Pi*, of a man who after a terrible shipwreck travelled the Pacific Ocean with a live tiger on a small boat and survived. After a year, he landed on the coast of Mexico where he started a new life. These stories from the news are not only quickly taken at face value but revered as

12. Edgar and Oliphint, *Christian Apologetics*, Vol. 2, 460.

13. Edgar and Oliphint, *Christian Apologetics*, Vol. 2, 461.

14. Edgar and Oliphint, *Christian Apologetics*, Vol. 2, 461.

amazing and as examples of what "people can do." Yet, when confronted with similar Bible accounts, they are quickly dismissed. There seems to be a double standard here. Why? It comes as a result of an atheistic bias that simply refuses to be acknowledged or resisted.

The job of the presuppositionalist is to aid in the discovery of this bias in a person's life. However, this must be accomplished with great care and love—not with a patronizing or degrading attitude. Sensibility, discernment, and love are a must. Then, with the presupposition that biblical accounts have not been proven to be fictitious, the foundation for a reasonable apologetics response can be laid.

Still, how does one implement freedom in Christ into the Pressupositionalist's school of thought? Why is this approach the most effective when dealing with Postmoderns? It is the most effective because it dispels their foundational belief in relativisms and naturalism. It can, however, be also challenging to help someone overcome their complete rejection of biblical inherency. There will be those for whom no matter how many sensible explanations are given, they will stubbornly prefer to deny. Sadly, for those individuals, very little can be done. However, it is for the sake of those who fall outside of this category that the efforts are worth their weight in gold.

For believers, the Bible is the ultimate manual for life. It explains how all creation came into existence and for what purpose, including that of humanity. More importantly, in the Bible one learns how to live. The Bible spells out both the rewards as well as the consequences of straying from God's prescribed way of living. Obedience leads to life and peace, while disobedience leads to misery and ultimately death. The peace offered by the freedom of Christ is yet another reward for obedience. The job of the apologist who assumes the truths of the Bible is therefore to show greater logic value in biblical truths than in naturalism. This can be accomplished by attesting to the reality to the unmistakable peace found in service and obedience to God and others. This is the definition of true freedom that can only be found in Christ.

The Church of Christ and Postmodernism

Undeniably, Postmodernism is the church's greatest challenge. Oddly, the job of the apologists is not to abandon a rigid, fundamentalist, unreasonable stand. Rather, the task is to bring the Postmodern to think about his foundational basis. To wit, the undertaking of apologetic evangelism is one directed to help unbelievers acknowledge their biases towards theistic writings while helping them overcome any faulty preconceived ideas. One must begin by showing not only the rationality of a theistic world but also its possibility and likelihood.

Because of the pervasive reliability on science as the bases for truth, the apologist's task here is twofold. First, the apologist must dispel the misconception that science and the Bible are contradictory. Rather, plenty of evidence points to the exact opposite. Science and the Bible are complementary, not opposed.[15] Finally, a more important question is warranted. It comes from Jean-Francois Lyotard's work, *The Post-Modern Condition.*[16]

In a way similar to the false idea of infinity regression, Lyotard questions the proofs provided via the scientific method. Speaking of those who are relaying on only the scientific method as the bases of truth, he asks, "What I say is true because I prove that it is . . . what proof is there that my proof is true?"[17] In other words, a further explanation is required to support the validity of the scientific method itself.[18] Namely, God's existence and His revelation through His Word are required.

The scientific method is sound, and it provides reliable information. Yet, it does not explain itself. It is critical that both believers and unbelievers accept both these truths. For believers, it is critical that they give due credit to the scientific method without dismissing God's sovereignty over it. For unbelievers, the same is true but in reverse order. This method, along with all other skills

---

15. Van der Merwe, "Rethinking the Message," 6.

16. Hynes, "Postmodernism and the Church," 74.

17. Hynes, "Postmodernism and the Church," 77.

18. Hynes, "Postmodernism and the Church," 77.

afforded by a person's God-given reason and intellect, do not stand on their own nor do they deny God. Instead, they complement each other and attest to the existence of a Creator who encourages intellectualism, science, and encourages discovery of new ideas.

This understanding brings freedom to both: those who embrace the crippling manifestation of extreme fundamentalism, and to those of the directly opposite yet equally radical view. The job of the apologist is to help seek understanding of the freedom found in the balance of these two opinions. It is just as freeing and critical for the church to not only understand but also embrace this position, as it is for unbelievers. As long as believers remain stuck on the naïve stance that the only way to prove their faith is to pretend that they need to only believe blindly in God, those to be evangelized will remain skeptical (and rightfully so). They have had enough nonsense.

A presuppositionalist apologist maintains that it is time to put aside all misconceptions of the irrationality of Scripture and embrace it as the highest level of rationality. This is the greatest expression of freedom in Christ.

CONCLUSION

THE GOAL OF THIS WORK has been twofold. Although the purpose of the study is to contribute to the field of apologetics, first an in-depth analysis revealing the true meaning of freedom in Christ was essential. With this understanding, apologists and believers alike will be better equipped to defend the Christian faith. It seemed appropriate to begin by examining freedom in Christ from the perspective of the Jews and of the Hebrew Scriptures, which account for more than 50% of the Christian Bible.

This introductory section led to two main conclusions: (1) upon examining the pattern of Scripture, freedom in Christ means fundamentally a permanent release from the subjugation of sin. Yet, this clarification is only but one half of the equation, for the liberation from sin's lordship is not simply for its own sake; rather, freedom in Christ has been bestowed for the purpose of submission and obedience to God; (2) freedom in Christ is not to be understood as a free pass for sinning so that the grace of God may abound. Christians who sin still need to repent. Therefore, although a Christian cannot lose his salvation, freedom in Christ does not mean that one may proudly continue to sin while his relationship with his brothers and sisters, and with God, remains unaffected.

Again, with the apologetics framework of this study in mind, the difference between Christian freedom and secular freedom was presented next. This purpose of that comparison was to eliminate any misunderstanding of the abysmal gap between the two.

Also, it was necessary to set up a fundamental understanding of the views of those who the apologist is aiming to reach. In this section, it was concluded that, in stark contrast to freedom in Christ, secular freedom is a pseudo-freedom that is in fact a manifestation of bondage. Those who seek the material things of this world for the sake of being free to do as they please are only but prisoners of their lifestyles—particularly if they are willing to do anything, including sinning to maintain it.

Next, an in-depth study of the prevalent worldview of Postmodernism revealed its most common fallacies unveiling a wealth of opportunities for apologists to respond. Post-Modernism is primarily characterized by its belief in the concept of relativism, naturalistic worldview, and antinomianism—the rejection of all metanarratives. To the Postmodern man, nothing or no one defines their reality but themselves. This section revealed not only the violation of the laws of logic that their views entail, but also how to understand their perspective. These two findings are vital in developing a good response to their arguments.

The last chapter was written for the purpose of implementing the priceless gift of freedom from sin into the different schools of thought in the field of apologetics. Apologetics contains many facets because it must be comprehensive and respond properly to a wide array of scenarios and perspectives. So, throughout history, it has been divided into several fields that are meant to respond in different ways to skeptics' protests and even to believers' questions.

The field of Classical Apologetics works on the framework of teleological arguments and the classical use of reason. In this arena, apologists use arguments from nature and reasoning to develop their arguments. The analogy of the birds best represents how freedom in Christ as the true purpose of humanity can be implemented into classical apologetics.

The animals are free, at least most people who look upon them envy them at times, wanting to be like them, free from responsibilities. Yet, all creatures have the responsibility to fulfill their purpose within the creation. The animals gladly do it, as can we—to the extent that humans can appreciate the freedom in their existence. Humans must learn to see how they, just like the birds of the sky, are only truly free when they have Christ and consequently the freedom to obey God and play their part in the creation. Then, they will be free like the rest of the world.

In the field of Reformed Apologetics, it was concluded that the purpose to the apologist is to assist the person in accepting God as the Creator and redeemer as the basis of his teleology. The specific reality in question relates to the understanding that man is not truly free until he has surrendered to the service of the Creator.

Finally, in the field of Presuppositionalism, the other two apologetics schools meet what seems to be the pinnacle of apologetic defense. Presuppositionalism assumes not only that the Word of God is true, but that living by it and accepting it is the greatest form of rationalism. Therefore, this school of thought in a way encompasses Classical and Reformed Apologetics. In this section, the peace of God was highlighted as the ultimate indicator of genuine freedom. This is, however, not attained until the individual accepts and understands Christ's gift of redemption and surrenders to God.

Christ's Atonement has afforded a limitless number of blessings to humanity, not the least of which is freedom from sin. Let the field of apologetics be the first to communicate to all people the priceless value of this gift.

BIBLIOGRAPHY

Augustine. *City of God, Volume VI: Books 18.36–20.* trans. William Chase Greene. Loeb Classical Library. Cambridge: Harvard University.

Alexander, J. N. "For Freedom Christ Has Set Us Free." *Sewanee Theological Review* 57.1 (2013) 73–76, 8.

Allen, Wayne. "Are the Liberal Movements in Judaism Really Modern?" *Modern Judaism* 33.1 (2013) 45–55.

Bahnsen, Greg, and Willem A. Vangemeren. *The Law, the Gospel, and the Modern Christian.* Grand Rapids: Zondervan, 1993.

Beilby, James K. *The Nature of the Atonement: Four Views.* Downers Grove: InterVarsity, 2006.

Blanton, Thomas R. "Saved by Obedience: Matthew 1:21 in Light of Jesus' Teaching on the Torah." *Journal of Biblical Literature* 132.2 (2013) 393–413.

Block, Daniel I., ed. *Israel: Ancient Kingdom or Late Invention?* Nashville: B&L, 2008.

Bock, Darrell. *Studying the Historical Jesus.* Grand Rapids: Baker Academic, 2002.

Burt, Sean. "Your Torah Is My Delight: Repetition and the Poetics of Immanence in Psalm 119." *Journal of Biblical Literature* 137.3 (2018) 685–700.

Brown, Callum G. "The Necessity of Atheism: Making Sense of Secularization." *Journal of Religious History* 41.4 (2017) 439–56.

Bush, L. Russ. *The Advancement, Keeping the Faith in an Evolutionary Age.* Tennessee: B&H, 2003.

Chilton, Bruce, and Craig Evans. *Practice: Jesus and the Torah the Gospels' Judaic Way of Life. Judaism in the New Testament Practices and Beliefs.* London: Routledge, 1995.

Choi, Junghwa. *Jewish Leadership in Roman Palestine from 70 C. E. to 135 C. E.* Leiden: Brill, 2013.

Conroy, K. "A New Spiritual Home: Progressive Christianity at the Grass-Roots." *Journal of Religion Health* 46 (2007) 169–70. https://doi-org.ezproxy.liberty.edu/10.1007/s10943-006-9096-8.

BIBLIOGRAPHY

Coolman, Holly Taylor. "Christological Torah." *Studies in Christian-Jewish Relations* 5.1 (2011, 2010) CP1–CP12.

De Gruchy, John. "Christian Humanism, Progressive Christianity, and Social Transformation." *Journal for the Study of Religion* 31.1 (2018) 54, 69, 331.

Duffield, Ian K. "Difficult Texts: Matthew 28:19–20." *Theology* 120.2 (2017) 108–11. https://doi.org/10.1177/0040571X16676673.

Dulles, Avery Cardinal. *A History of Apologetics.* San Francisco: Ignatius, 1999.

Eaton, Mark. "Review of *Christian Fundamentalism and the Culture of Disenchantment*, by Paul Maltby." *College Literature* 41.3 (2014) 133–36. doi:10.1353/lit.2014.0036.

Edgar, William, and K. Scott Oliphint, ed. *Christian Apologetics: Past and Present.* 2 vols. Wheaton, IL: Crossway, 2009.

Edles, Laura Desfor. "Contemporary Progressive Christianity and Its Symbolic Ramifications." *Cultural Sociology* 7.1 (2013) 3–22. doi:10.1177-1749975512453659.

Epstein, Gil S., and Ira N. Gang. "Understanding the Development of Fundamentalism." *Public Choice* 132.¾ (2007) 257–71.

Featherstone, Mike. *Consumer Culture and Postmodernism.* 2nd ed. Thousand Oaks: SAGE, 2007.

Ferziger, Adam S. "Fluidity and Bifurcation: Critical Biblical Scholarship and Orthodox Judaism in Israel and North America." *Modern Judaism* 39.3 (2019) 233–70.

Frantisek, Abel. "Freedom in Christ in Galatians: A Matter of Identity." *Communio Viatorum* 61.3 (2019) 235–55.

Gager, John G. *Reinventing Paul.* New York: Oxford University Press, 1992.

Graff, Gil. "Giving Voice to "Torah-True Judaism" in the U.S, 1922–39: Leo Jung and the Legacy of the Rabbiner Seminar." *Modern Judaism* 34.2 (2014) 167–72.

Habermas, Gary R., and Michael R. Licona. *The Case for the Resurrection of Jesus.* Grand Rapids: Kregel, 2004.

Hartog, Paul. "The Christology of the Martyrdom of Polycarp: Martyrdom as Both Imitation of Christ and Election by Christ." *Perichoresis: The Theological Journal of Emanuel University* 12.2 (2014) 137–52.

Hynes, Timothy. "Postmodernism and the Church: An Opportunity and a Challenge." *The Journal of Theology* 6.2 (2016) 67–85.

Iles Johnston, Sarah, ed. *Ancient Religions: Beliefs and Rituals across the Mediterranean World.* Cambridge: Harvard University Press, 2007.

Jervis, L. Ann. *Galatians.* Grand Rapids: Baker, 1993.

Joslyn-Siemiatkoski, Daniel. "Moses Received the Torah at Sinai and Handed It on" (Mishnah Avot 1:1): The Relevance of the Written and Oral Torah for Christians." *Anglican Theological Review* 91.3 (2009) 443–66.

Kister, Manahem. "Romans 5:12–21 Against the Background of Torah-Theology and Hebrew Usage." *Harvard Theological Review* 100.4 (2007) 391–424.

Knox, John S. *Sacro-Egoism: The Rise of Religious Individualism in the West.* Eugene, OR: Wipf & Stock, 2016.

Lewis, C. S. *The Abolition of Man.* New York: HarperOne, 2001.

Lewis, Tyson E. "Studying Postmodernism," *Educational Philosophy and Theory* 50.14 (2018) 1342–43. https://doi-org.ezproxy.liberty.edu/10.1080/00131 857.2018.1458792.

Lioy, Dan. *Jesus As Torah in John 1–12.* Eugene, OR: Wipf & Stock, 2007.

McHale, Brian. *The Cambridge Introduction to Postmodernism.* Cambridge: Cambridge University Press, 2015.

Moo, Douglas J. *2 Peter, and Jude: From Biblical Text to Contemporary Life.* Grand Rapids: Zondervan, 1996.

Niall, Lucy, et al. *A Dictionary of Postmodernism.* 1st ed. Chichester: Wiley-Blackwell, 2016.

Nystrom, David P. *James.* Grand Rapids: HarperCollins, 1997.

O'Callaghan, Paul. "Is the Christian Believer Conservative or Liberal?" *Church Communication and Culture* 4.2 (2019) 137–51.

Pancaro, Severino. *The Law in the Fourth Gospel: The Torah and the Gospel, Moses and Jesus, Judaism and Christianity According to John.* Leiden: Brill, 1975.

Pollack, Detlef, and Gert Pickel. "Religious Individualization or Secularization? Testing Hypotheses of Religious Change – The Case of Eastern and Western Germany." *The British Journal of Sociology* 58.4 (2007) 603–32. https://doi-org.ezproxy.liberty.edu/10.1111/j.1468-4446.2007.00168.x.

Raisanen, Heikki, and David E. Orton. *Jesus, Paul and Torah: Collected Essays,* Vol. 43. 1st ed. London: JSOT, 1992.

Rogers, Katherin A. "Christ's Freedom: Anselm vs Molina." *Religious Studies* 52.4 (2016) 497–512.

Schaeffer, Francis A. *Escape From Reason.* Downers Grove: InterVarsity, 2006.

Scherman, Nosson, and Meir Zlotowitz. *The Ohel Sarah Women's Siddur.* Art Scroll Series. Klein Edition. Brooklyn: Mesorah, 2018.

Tapie, Matthew. "Christ, Torah, and the Faithfulness of God: The Concept of Supersessionism in 'The Gifts and the Calling.'" *Studies in Christian-Jewish Relations* 12.1 (2017) 1–18.

Van der Merwe, Dirk G. "Rethinking the Message of the Church in the 21st Century: An Amalgamation between Science and Religion." *Hervormde Teologiese Studies* 75.4 (2019) 1–9.

Van Vlastuin, Willem. "Complementary Apologetics: An Attempt for the Integration of Apologetic Schools." *Die Skriflig: Tydskrif Ven Die Gereformeerde Teologiese Vereniging* 50.1 (2016) 1–9.

Viljoen, Francois P. "The Matthean Jesus' Surprising Instruction to Obey the Teachers of the Law and the Pharisees." *Hervormde Teologiese Studies* 74.1 (2018) 1–10.

Wilkens, Steve. *Faith and Reason: Three Views.* Downers Grove: InterVarsity, 2014.

Williams, John. "Christianity in the Modern World: Changes and Controversies." *International Journal of Christianity and Education* 22.1 (2018) 87–89. https://doi.org/10.1177/2056997117743953.

Wolin, Richard. *The Seduction of Unreason: The Intellectual Romance with Fascism From Nietzsche to Postmodernism.* Princeton: Princeton University Press, 2006.

INDEX

Index

www.ingramcontent.com/pod-product-compliance
Lightning Source LLC
Chambersburg PA
CBHW060418090426
42734CB00011B/2357